Iqbal's concept of God

D1744750

Iqbal's concept of God

M. S. Raschid

KPI

LONDON, NEW YORK, SYDNEY and HENLEY

First published in 1981.
This edition published in 1986 by KPI Limited
14 Leicester Square, London WC2H 7PH, England

Distributed by
Routledge & Kegan Paul plc
14 Leicester Square, London WC2H 7PH, England

Routledge & Kegan Paul Inc
29 West 35th Street, New York, NY 10001, USA

Routledge & Kegan Paul
c/o Methuen Law Book Company
44 Waterloo Road
North Ryde, NSW 2113
Australia

Routledge & Kegan Paul plc
Broadway House, Newtown Road,
Henley-on-Thames, Oxon RG9 1EN, England

Set in Press Roman
by Hope Services Abingdon
and printed in Great Britain
by St Edmundsbury Press,
Bury St Edmunds, Suffolk

ISBN 0-7103-0187-1

Contents

Acknowledgments

It is a pleasure and privilege to record my profound indebtedness to my learned and distinguished teachers, Professor W. H. Walsh, Professor H. D. Lewis and Professor E. G. Parrinder. I also wish to express my gratitude to Professor Muhsin Mahdi of Harvard, President of the Society for the Study of Islamic Philosophy and Science, for his interest and for requesting Professor Fazlur Rahman, Professor of Islamic Thought at the University of Chicago, to read the work. I am deeply grateful to the latter for his most scrupulous reading and assessment. Thanks are due to my friends Jamal Islam and Absar Ahmad for their support and encouragement during the difficult period when I was engaged in research on Iqbal. Very special thanks to Qamar for her tender care and attention at the critical, and final, stage of the work. My greatest indebtedness is to Safia Haroon Raschid.

In the Name of God,
the Most Gracious, the Dispenser of Grace

We beseech God, in the name of His greatness which transcends all limits, and His munificence which outruns all measures:

To pour upon us the light of guidance, and to remove from us the darkness of ignorance and wrong-doing;

To make us like those who saw truth as truth, and chose to follow it; and those who saw falsehood as falsehood, and decided to eschew it;

To bestow upon us the felicity which He has promised to His saints and prophets;

To initiate us, on our departure from the House of Delusion, into that happiness the height of which cannot be scanned by the understanding, and the extent of which cannot be conjured up by the imagination;

To give us, when after deliverance from the horrors of the Doomsday we approach the bliss of Paradise, 'that which no eye ever saw, no ear ever heard, and which never occurred to the heart of man'; and

To invest with peace and bless our Prophet Muhammad, the Chosen one, the best one of all mankind; and his noble descendants and pure companions, who were the keys to guidance, and the lamps lit in darkness.

From the Introduction to Al-Ghazali's
Tahafut al-Falasifah
(*The Incoherence of*
the Philosophers)

To the memory of my father,
M. A. Raschid of Burma (1912–78);

May the mercy of God be upon him

To my mother and brother
and to
Safia Haroon Raschid and
Rose Tin Tin Sann Raschid:
in honour, and with love and gratitude

Introduction and summary

This small work makes a large claim: in it the received opinion of Sir Muhammad Iqbal (1877-1938) as a great religious *thinker* is challenged. Iqbal provides a good point of departure for the assessment and development of contemporary Islamic thought.[1] Professor Fazlur Rahman, in the course of a fair and balanced appraisal of Iqbal, has expressed the view that 'the tension between Wesernism and Islamic fundamentalism in Indian Islam has produced one outstanding figure, that of Sir Muhammad Iqbal, the most serious Muslim philosophical thinker of modern times'.[2] Generally, however, quite extravagant claims have been made for Iqbal. The following two instances are typical of the excessively adulatory and uncritical attitude of Muslim scholars in the Indian subcontinent:[3]

> There is no doubt that Iqbal is the most versatile genius that the modern Muslim world has produced.[4]

> Iqbal occupies a unique position in the history of Muslim thought, for he is the first great thinker of Islam who has made a serious attempt to reconstruct Islamic philosophy on an existential basis, without ignoring the claims of reason to critically examine the results of intuitive experience . . . what Ghazali had failed to do, Iqbal accomplished.[5]

Somewhat paradoxically, such glib and unwarranted estimates are the result of a situation alluded to by Iqbal himself in the following words: 'During the last five hundred years religious thought in Islam has been practically stationary. There was a time when European thought received inspiration from the world of Islam.'[6] It is outside my scope here to go into the complex nature and causes of this process of cultural decline.

Suffice it now to say that I believe that its real roots are a deep and pervasive process of spiritual, and consequently also moral, degeneration throughout the Muslim world.

Iqbal himself is modest about the nature and purpose of his work. Referring to 'the demand for a scientific form of religious knowledge,' he writes:[7]

> In these lectures . . . I have tried to meet, even though partially, this urgent demand by attempting to reconstruct Muslim religious philosophy with due regard to the philosophical tradition of Islam and the more recent developments in the various domains of human knowledge. . . . It must, however, be remembered that there is no such thing as finality in philosophical thinking. As knowledge advances and fresh avenues of thought are opened, other views, and probably sounder views than those set forth in these lectures, are possible. Our duty is carefully to watch the progress of human thought, and to maintain an independent critical attitude towards it.

The scope of this work is limited, almost exclusively, to an examination of Iqbal's thought about God in what is, perhaps arguably, the most centrally important and interesting chapter, from both the theological and philosophical point of view, of *The Reconstruction of Religious Thought in Islam*: chapter II, 'The philosophical test of the revelations of religious experience'. This provides a fair sample of Iqbal's work as a religious thinker. I submit, on the basis of the evidence presented here, that the claim that Iqbal is a major religious thinker cannot be vindicated. Of course, this in no way detracts from his stature as one of the principal figures, together with Sir Sayyid Ahmad Khan and the Maulana Abul-Kalam Azad, who inspired the modern resurgence and reawakening of subcontinental Islam. It is outside my scope and competence to try to assess Iqbal as a poet and literary figure.

A note about the arrangement of this work is in order here. It is divided into three parts. The examination of chapter II of *The Reconstruction of Religious Thought in Islam* takes up the whole of part I of this book. I have tried to follow the actual sequence of Iqbal's own thoughts — the beginning and the transitions are somewhat abrupt: hence, up to a point, the presentation may appear rather disjointed in places. There is, however, an underlying unity of theme and purpose and this is brought out in the 'overall critique' I have provided towards the end of part I (pp. 36-8). The Hegelian influence on Iqbal was a particularly tricky theme to handle in a limited compass — especially as, to the best of my knowledge, it has not been shown before by any scholar.

This influence was thought to be important enough to justify some extended discussion of Hegel, including a separate chapter designed to exhibit schematically the nature and scope of his system. There is, of course, good *external* evidence for the Hegelian impact on Iqbal, and this is easily related to his Cambridge period (*circa* 1905-7) with J.M.E. McTaggart.[8] The precise nature and implications of Iqbal's doctrine of God are spelled out in part II: 'Iqbal and the Muslim tradition', His concept of God is seen here in the context of the orthodox Muslim doctrine, as well as that formulated in the Sufi (Islamic mystical) tradition; there is a quite unexpected, and paradoxical, affinity with the latter.[9] Iqbal's attempt to adduce Quranic support for his case is also examined in this part. The inquiry is carried further, in a philosophical sense, in part III: 'Beyond Iqbal: the nature of the problem of God'. The references in part III to Iqbal, Ahmad Sirhindi and al-Ghazali are meant to maintain the link with the Muslim tradition.

The argument of this book may be summarised as follows. The development of Iqbal's concept of God is examined and assessed. His concept of God is a finite (panentheistic) one, and is arrived at largely by a superficial and uncritical reading of western science and philosophy. The chief philosophical influences are those of Hegel, Whitehead and Bergson. There is both misunderstanding as well as distortion, no doubt unconscious, on Iqbal's part. The weakest part of his case is the bold, but quite illegitimate, attempt to draw extravagant metaphysical conclusions from his reading of these western thinkers. He provides virtually no original, or even independent, argumentation.

Iqbal tries to relate his metaphysical extrapolations from western sources — especially his finite concept of God — to the *Quran* and the tradition of Muslim thought. This enterprise is equally unsuccessful. In particular, his attitude to the *Quran* is extremely irresponsible and he manages to ignore the whole tradition of *tafsir* (exegesis) and *kalam* (theology). It is argued that Iqbal's finite deity cannot be reconciled with the supremely transcendent, but also immanent, God of the *Quran*. His *panentheistic* notion of God is very close to the *pantheistic* Sufi concept of God: this is paradoxical as the fundamental premises of Iqbal and the Sufis are very different. The Sufi doctrine of God is examined in its contemporary form, as expounded and defended by Isa Nuruddin (Frithjof Schuon) and Abubakr Sirajuddin (Martin Lings); it is found that *it*, too, is irreconcilable with the orthodox Quranic doctrine. The examination of the Sufi teaching of *Wahdat al-Wujud* (Oneness of Being) raises the complex and difficult question of mystical experience and its conceptual or doctrinal interpretation. The discussion of this issue centres around the writing of the contemporary philosopher, W.T. Stace; its conclusion is that the erroneous formulation of the Sufis is the result of a failure to make the all-important distinction between mystical experience and interpretation.

Finally, an attempt is made to go beyond Iqbal and to specify quite precisely the *logical* peculiarity of the problem of God. The implications of this position for the nature of our knowledge of God, specifically in the areas of revelation and mysticism, are explored briefly and tentatively. Reference is made, in addition to Iqbal, to the ideas of Ahmad Sirhindi and al-Ghazali.

All references to *The Reconstruction of Religious Thought in Islam* — hereafter referred to simply as *The Reconstruction* — are to the Lahore (Ashraf) edition, dated merely as 'reprinted March 1958'. The pagination differs from that of the Oxford edition of 1934, now out of print.

M.S.R.

Part I

Iqbal and the western tradition

European culture, on its intellectual side, is only a further development of some of the most important phases of the culture of Islam. Our only fear is that the dazzling exterior of European culture may arrest our movement and we may fail to reach the true inwardness of that culture. During all the centuries of our intellectual stupor Europe has been seriously thinking on the great problems in which the philosophers and scientists of Islam were so keenly interested. Since the Middle Ages, when the schools of Muslim theology were completed, infinite advance has taken place in the domain of human thought and experience.

Sir Muhammad Iqbal, *The Reconstruction of Religious Thought in Islam*

Chapter 1

The arguments for the existence of God

1.1

Iqbal writes: 'Scholastic philosophy has put forward three arguments for the existence of God. These arguments, known as the Cosmological, the Teleological, and the Ontological, embody a real movement of thought in its quest after the Absolute.'(p. 28)[1] The Hegelian influence is already evident from the mention of 'the Absolute'. The opening paragraph concludes with the dual assertion that the arguments lack logical rigour, 'and further betray a rather superficial interpretation of experience'.

Iqbal's treatment of the three arguments is extremely brief. 'The Cosmological argument views the world as a finite effect, and passing through a series of dependent sequences, related as causes and effects, stops at an uncaused first cause, because of the unthinkability of an infinite regress' (p. 28). His objections are as follows: (1) A finite effect can only yield a finite cause, or an infinite series of such causes. 'To elevate one member of the series to the dignity of an uncaused first cause' is to nullify the very law of causation upon which the whole argument rests. (2) The first cause necessarily excludes its effect. Thus the effect, in setting a limit to its own cause, reduces it to something finite. (3) The first cause cannot be regarded as a necessary being, for the two items in the cause-effect relation are equally necessary to each other. (4) The necessity of existence is not identical with the conceptual necessity of causation, the latter being 'the utmost that this argument can prove'. Iqbal's markedly Hegelian summing-up is noteworthy (pp. 28-9):

> The argument really tries to reach the infinite by merely negating the finite but the infinite reached by contradicting the finite is a false

3

infinite which neither explains itself nor the finite which is thus made to stand in opposition to the infinite. The true infinite does not exclude the finite; it embraces the finite without effacing its finitude, and explains and justifies its being.

He concludes: 'Logically speaking, then, the movement from the finite to the infinite as embodied in the Cosmological argument is quite illegitimate; and the argument fails *in toto*.'

The teleological argument 'scrutinises the effect with a view to discover the character of its cause. From the traces of foresight, purpose, and adaptation in nature, it infers the existence of a self-conscious being of infinite intelligence and power' (p. 29). To this, Iqbal objects that, 'At best, it gives us a skilful external contriver working on a pre-existing dead and intractable material.' Thus the argument yields only a contriver and not a creator. The situation is analogous to that of a human designer – the designer is both external to, as well as limited by, his material; in other words, he is a finite designer. This conclusion results, in Iqbal's view, from the fallacious nature of the proposed analogy: 'There is really no analogy between the work of the human artificer and the phenomena of nature.' Whereas 'the human artificer' works by selecting and removing his materials from their natural context 'nature, however, constitutes a system of wholly interdependent members'. Again, there is a definite Hegelian tone.

The ontological argument (p. 30):

> The Cartesian form of the argument runs thus: 'To say that an attribute is contained in the nature or in the concept of a thing is the same as to say that the attribute is true of this thing and that it may be affirmed to be in it. But necessary existence is contained in the nature of the concept of God. Hence it may be with truth affirmed that necessary existence is in God, or that God exists.' Descartes supplements this argument by another. We have the idea of a perfect being in our mind. What is the source of the idea? It cannot come from nature, for nature exhibits nothing but change. It cannot create the idea of a perfect being. Therefore corresponding to the idea in our minds there must be an objective counterpart which is the cause of the idea of a perfect being in our mind.

Iqbal observes that the argument is similar to the cosmological argument. 'But whatever may be the form of the argument, it is clear that the conception of existence is no proof of objective existence.' Kant's criticism with his example of the two hundred dollars (*sic*), is recalled (p. 30):

All that the argument proves is that the idea of a perfect being includes the *idea* of his existence. Between the idea of a perfect being in my mind and the objective existence of that being there is a gulf which cannot be bridged over by a transcendental act of thought. The argument, as stated, is in fact a *petitio principii*; for it takes for granted the very point in question, i.e., the transition from the logical to the real.

Iqbal now concludes, confidently 'that the Ontological and the Teleological arguments, as ordinarily stated, carry us nowhere. And the reason of their failure is that they look upon "thought" as an agency working on things from without.'

1.2

Iqbal's subsequent elaboration on this theme amounts to a major statement of his position. It deserves to be quoted in full (p. 31):

This view of thought gives us a mere mechanician in the one case, and creates an unbridgeable gulf between the ideal and the real in the other. It is, however, possible to take thought not as a principle which organises and integrates its material from the outside, but as a potency which is formative of the very being of its material. Thus regarded thought or idea is not alien to the original nature of things; it is the ultimate ground and constitutes the very essence of their being, infusing in them from the very beginning of their career and inspiring their onward march to a self-determined end. But our present situation necessitates the dualism of thought and being. Every act of human knowledge bifurcates what might on proper enquiry turn out to be a unity into a self that knows and a confronting "other" that is known. That is why we are forced to regard the object that confronts the self as something existing in its own right, external to and independent of the self whose act of knowledge makes no difference to the object known. The true significance of the Ontological and the Teleological arguments will appear only if we are able to show that the human situation is not final and that thought and being are ultimately one.

This statement contains, or at least assumes, a whole epistemology and an entire metaphysic − in fact, the epistemology and metaphysic of Hegel.[2]

1.3

Before proceeding further we must take careful note of Iqbal's general conclusion at this stage of his thesis. He asserts (as quoted above) that the true significance of the ontological and the teleological arguments will appear only when we demonstrate the ultimate unity of thought and being. Further, he maintains that this will be possible only if we 'examine and interpret experience, following the clue furnished by the Quran which regards experience within and without as symbolic of a reality described by it, as "the First and the Last, the visible and the invisible" ' (p. 31).

Is Iqbal's statement of the three arguments adequate? Are his own arguments original? If so, are they cogent? These three related questions will be considered in the context of the development, and specifically the Hegelian development, of the arguments within the western philosophical tradition. For the moment we need only remark that Iqbal's treatment of this difficult and complex problem is so superficial (perhaps because so brief) as to be almost cavalier.

Chapter 2

Hegel

2.1

The Hegelian influence is clear both in Iqbal's criticism of the cosmological argument, as well as in his combined criticism of the ontological and teleological arguments. Despite the observation above, that Iqbal's comments on the ontological and teleological arguments contain a whole epistemology and an entire metaphysic, his position is, at best, only quasi-Hegelian. Indeed, we must even remain open to the possibility that it is no more than *pseudo*-Hegelian. Some of the most profound and complex epistemological and metaphysical problems in the western philosophical tradition have been dealt with in a distressingly glib and a disconcertingly rapid fashion. The situation is ominous and raises disquieting questions about the author's philosophical credentials and competence. (Perhaps it is symptomatic of Iqbal's whole attitude and approach.)

2.2

A careful reading of such centrally relevant Hegel texts as the various well-known prefaces and introductions to some of his works and the *Lectures on the Proofs of God's Existence*, together with the works of such modern scholars as Collins, Fackenheim, Findlay and Soll, reveal alike the unprecedentedly ambitious character, uncompromising subtlety and extreme complexity of the Hegelian philosophy.[1] Hence the existence of rival bodies of expositors and interpreters – from *transcendent* (right wing) to *immanent* (left wing). When we juxtapose Iqbal's brief comments to this body of philosophical writing and commentary an

7

acutely embarrassing situation ensues. Indeed, we are constrained to ask, 'Does Iqbal understand Hegel?' To this question we must now turn. Consider now the following two statements by Iqbal:

(1) Apropos the cosmological argument: 'The true infinite does not exclude the finite; it embraces the finite without effacing its finitude, and explains and justifies its being.' (See p. 4)

(2) Apropos the ontological and teleological arguments: '. . . thought or idea is not alien to the original nature of things; it is the ultimate ground and constitutes the very essence of their being, infusing in them from the very beginning of their career and inspiring their onward march to a self-determined end.' (See the whole passage, above, p. 5, from which this extract is taken.)

The Hegelian influence is unmistakable and it is remarkable that Hegel is not explicitly mentioned. This suggestion of an Hegelian influence is therefore an interpretation, but in its absence Iqbal's statements are not intelligible. In the present climate of English-speaking philosophy, statements of the character 'The true infinite does not exclude the finite' and 'thought is the ultimate ground of the original nature of things and constitutes the very essence of their being' would at least raise, and left unqualified perhaps deserve, considerable suspicion and incredulity; indeed, the more positivistically inclined linguistic philosopher would hardly hesitate in branding them as patent nonsense. The complexion of this problem is radically altered when we attempt to understand Iqbal's statements within the context of the Hegelian system. My aim here is the very modest one of trying to make sense of Iqbal's arguments in the context of Hegel's philosophy. Clearly, then, we are committed to some minimum exposition of that philosophy, but I must emphasise that this 'minimum exposition' is not intended to be a condensed account of the Hegelian system. It is simply an attempt to indicate certain salient features in their barest outline so that we may get a reasonable view of the nature and purpose of the Hegelian philosophy — and sufficient, hopefully, to show that Iqbal's theses are intelligible only as integral components of such a system.

2.3 The Hegelian system

1 Hegel's circle

The Hegelian philosophy is, arguably, the most ambitious system developed within the western tradition. It presents at its very core the apparent paradox of setting out to resolve that which, in ordinary thought and experience, is irresolvable, to unite that which cannot be united: god and man, spirit and nature, thought and being, subject and object. It is a self-contained circle — an oft-recurring image throughout Hegel's writings — and one which is unprecedented alike in its comprehensiveness as well as its immunity to *external* criticism.[2] Hegel himself characterises his enterprise in the introduction (following the famous preface) to *The Phenomenology of Mind*:[3]

the pathway of the natural consciousness which is striving toward a true knowledge, or path of the soul which is making its way through the sequence of its own transformations as through way stations prescribed to it by its very nature, that it may, by purifying itself, lift itself to the level of Spirit and attain cognizance of what it is in itself through the completed experience of its own self.

For Hegel, philosophical truth cannot be merely stated, asserted, or even, in the traditional manner, argued for or demonstrated. Truth is rather the culmination of a long, arduous and complex process of development — the whole elaborate movement being subsumed (though not simply cancelled) in the final result. Accordingly, such terms as 'emerge', 'the final outcome', 'consummation', assume a special significance and occur frequently in his writings.[4] The following rigorously selected textual utterances well indicate the nature and style of the Hegelian philosophy.

From the preface to *The Phenomenology of Mind* (W. Kauffmann, *Hegel*, 1966)
This becoming of science in general or of knowledge is what this phenomenology of the spirit represents .... To become true knowledge, to generate the element of science which is a pure concept itself, it has to work its way through a long journey'. (p. 400)

Later on, in the same section:

The individual must also pass through the contents of the educational stages of the general spirit ... (p. 402)

The world spirit has had the patience to pass through these forms in the long expanse of time, taking upon itself the tremendous labour of world history.... (p. 404)

And further:

Consciousness knows and comprehends nothing but what lies within its experience. . . . The Spirit, however, becomes an object, for the Spirit is this movement of becoming something other for itself, i.e., an object for its self, and then to sublimate this otherhood. And experience is the name we give to just this movement. . . . (p. 412)

Science may organise itself only through the life of the Concept [a key Hegelian term: *Begriff* – translated as The Concept or The Notion] ; the determinedness which some would take externally from the schema to affix it to existence is in science, the self-moving soul of the abundant content. (p. 432) [A related statement occurs at the very beginning of the conclusion: 'I find the distinctive mark of science in the self-movement of the Concept. . . .' (p. 456)]

Further variations on this theme:

What therefore matters in the study of science is taking upon oneself the exertion of the Concept. . . . The content should be made to move itself by virtue of its own nature, i.e., through the self as its own self, and then to contemplate this movement. One should not intrude into the immanent rhythm of the Concept. . . . (p. 440)

The Concept is the object's own self which presents itself as its becoming. . . it is the Concept that moves itself and takes its determinations back into itself. In this movement the resting subject itself perishes. . . . (p. 442)

The return of the Concept into itself must be represented expressly. This movement which takes the place of that which proof was once supposed to accomplish is the dialectical movement of the proposition itself. (p. 448)

The following statements occur near the end of the preface:

True thoughts and scientific insight are to be won only through the work of the Concept. (p. 454)
We must have the conviction that it is of the nature of truth to prevail when its time has come, and that truth appears only when its time has come. . . . (p. 456)
From the introduction to *The Phenomenology of Mind*
This *dialectical* movement, which consciousness exercises on itself – on its knowledge as well as its object – is, insofar as *the new, true object emerges to consciousness* as the result of it, precisely that which is called *experience* (from M. Heidegger, *Hegel's Concept of Experience*, p. 23).

From *The Science of Logic*
This spiritual movement which, in its simple undifferentiatedness, gives itself its own determinedness and in its determinedness its equality with itself, which therefore is the immanent development of the Notion, this movement is the absolute method of knowing and at the same time is the immanent soul of the content itself. I maintain that it is this self-construing method alone which enables philosophy to be an objective, demonstrated science. (p. 28)

What logic is cannot be stated beforehand, rather does this knowledge of what it is first emerge as the final outcome and consummation of the whole exposition. . . . The Notion of logic has its genesis in the course of the exposition. (p. 43)

Now if logic has not undergone any change since Aristotle . . . then surely the conclusion which should be drawn is that it is all the more in need of a total reconstruction; for the Spirit, after its labours over two thousand years, must have attained to a higher consciousness about its thinking and about its own pure, essential nature. (p. 51)

The exposition of what alone can be the true method of philosophical science falls within the treatment of logic itself; for the method is the consciousness of the form of the inner self-movement of the content of logic. (p. 53)

Some of the features exemplified above, together with the image of the circle, are vigorously, and not ineloquently, expressed by Hegel in the section headed 'With what must the science begin?' at the beginning of *The Science of Logic* (p. 71):

Absolute Spirit which reveals itself as a concrete and final supreme truth of all being, and which at the *end* of the development is known as freely externalising itself, abandoning itself to the shape of an *immediate being* — opening or unfolding itself (*sich entschliessend*) into the creation of a world which contains all that fell into the development which preceded that result and which through this reversal of its position relatively to its beginning is transformed into something dependent on the result as principle. The essential requirement for the Science of Logic is not so much that the beginning be a pure immediacy, but rather that the whole of the science be within itself a circle in which the first is also the last and the last is also the first. . . . Thus the beginning of philosophy is the foundation which is present and preserved throughout the entire subsequent development, remaining completely immanent in its further determinations.

2 The nature of the content

According to Hegel religion and philosophy have the same content.[5] The following statement is especially worthy of note (introduction to *The Science of Logic*, p. 50):

> Logic is to be understood as the system of pure reason, as the realm of pure thought. This realm is truth as it is without veil and in its own absolute nature. It can therefore be said that this content is the exposition of God as he is in his eternal essence before the creation of nature and a finite mind.

Again, even more plainly, in the very opening section of the *Encyclopaedia Logic* (*The Logic of Hegel*) Hegel writes: 'The objects of philosophy, it is true, are upon the whole the same as those of religion. In both the subject is Truth, in that supreme sense in which God and God only is the Truth' (p. 3).

Further, Hegel identifies logic with the metaphysics. Thus in the preface to the first edition of *The Science of Logic* he writes of 'the Science of Logic which constitutes metaphysics proper or purely speculative philosophy'. And again, in the *Encyclopaedia Logic* (section 24): '*Logic therefore coincides with Metaphysics, the science of things set and held in thoughts*' (p. 45).

3 The elements of the system

The concept of the Notion (or the Concept: *Begriff*) is perhaps the most centrally important idea in the entire Hegelian philosophy. The last chapter of the *Encyclopaedia Logic* (chapter ix, third sub-division of logic, 'The doctrine of the Notion') commences thus: 'The Notion is the principle of freedom, the power of substance self-realised. It is a systematic whole'; and, further on (pp. 287-9):

> The **Notion**, in short, is what contains all the earlier categories of thought merged in it. It certainly is a form, but an infinite and creative form, which includes, but at the same time releases from itself, the fullness of all content . . . The Notion is a true concrete; for the reason that it involves Being and Essence, and the total wealth of these two spheres with them, merged in the unity of thought. . . .
> The movement of the Notion is *development*: by which that only is explicit which is already implicitly present.

If the spirit of the whole Hegelian philosophy could somehow be expressed briefly and schematically it is arguable that the most succinct formula would be 'the internal self-movement of the Notion'. This process of self-movement is the famous dialectic — the process through which Spirit undergoes self-negation and self-reconciliation (by *overreaching* its self-negated form). *Being*, the *Notion, dialectic, negation* and *overreaching* are, in fact, the key terms in the Hegelian system.[6] The three major components of the system are Logic, Nature and Spirit. Emil Fackenheim's brilliant work,[7] *The Religious Dimension in Hegel's Thought*, enunciates 'the principle of the Hegelian middle' — 'And we shall seek to grasp it by interpreting Hegel's thought as a threefold mediation, of which each phase involves the other two. Elements of all three phases are found scattered throughout Hegel's works' (p. 84). Fackenheim elaborates on this and goes on to quote the Hegelian passage which 'states the principle of the threefold mediation clearly, tersely, and completely' (p. 84). The passage opens thus (p. 84):

> Everything rational shows itself to be a threefold union or syllogism, in that each of the members takes the place both of one of the extremes and the mediating middle. This is especially the case with the three members of philosophical science, i.e., the logical Idea, Nature and Spirit.

4 The nature of the problem of knowledge

Hegel had the very deep insight that there could be no 'external' examination of knowledge. Therefore anything like the Kantian beginning is entirely mistaken. He writes in *The Science of Logic* (preface to the second edition, p. 36):

> Since, therefore, subjective thought is our very own, innermost act, and the objective notion of things constitutes their essential import, we cannot go outside this our act, we cannot stand above it, and just as little can we go beyond the nature of things.

Again, in the *Encyclopaedia Logic* (p. 17):

> But the examination of knowledge can only be carried out by an act of knowledge. To examine this so-called instrument is the same thing as to know it. But to seek to know before we know is as absurd as the wise resolution of Scholasticus, not to venture into the water until he had learned to swim.

Accordingly, the assessment of knowledge must necessarily remain a purely 'internal' procedure. Thus he writes in the introduction to *The Phenomenology of Mind*: 'The fundamental standard of measurement would lie in us . . . since consciousness provides itself with its own standard, investigation will be a comparison of consciousness with its own self' (quoted in Heidegger, *Hegel's Concept of Experience*, pp. 18-20). Hegel then develops this argument, and resolves the problem of the correspondence between knowledge and that (object) which is known, in terms of his concept of the Notion (*Begriff*). A modern scholar (K. R. Dove, *The Review of Metaphysics*, vol. 23, no. 4, June 1970) has characterised this phase of Hegel's thought as a revolutionary departure from the time-honoured approach to the problem of knowledge (based on the abstract distinction between knowledge and truth).

2.4

This rapid excursus into Hegel's philosophy enables us to return to the two Hegelian themes in Iqbal (*viz*. the unity of thought and being, and the finite-infinite relationship) more profitably.

1 The unity of thought and being

Ivan Soll has argued (*An Introduction to Hegel's Metaphysics*, 1969) that the abolition of the separation of the knowing subject from its object is the major function of *The Phenomenology of Mind*. There can be no doubt that this is one of the most important motifs in the entire Hegelian system. Soll relates this to Hegel's case against Kant: 'According to Hegel, the denial of knowledge of things-in-themselves rests on the separation of the knowing subject from its object.'[8]

Thus we read in the preface to *The Phenomenology of Mind*: 'It is the standpoint of consciousness to know of objective things in opposition to itself, and to know of itself in opposition to them' (quoted in Kauffmann, *Hegel*, p. 398). The development of philosophical science, through the internal self-movement of the Concept, overcomes this dichotomy (pp. 412, 414):

> Being is mediated absolutely; it is substantial content which is just as immediately property of the ego, *self-like*, or Concept. With this the Phenomenology of the Spirit is concluded. What the spirit prepares for itself in this phenomenology is the element of knowledge. In this element the moments of the spirit spread themselves out in the form of simplicity which knows its object as itself. They no longer fall apart into the opposition of being and knowledge but abide in the simplicity of knowledge.

In *The Science of Logic* we find plainer and more forceful statements
of these theses (p. 45):

> These views on the relation of subject and object to each other ex-
> press the determinations which constitute the nature of our ordinary,
> phenomenal consciousness; but when these prejudices are carried out
> into the sphere of reason . . . then they are errors the refutation of
> which throughout every part of the spiritual and natural universe is
> *philosophy*.

And further — Logic is (p. 60):

> defined as the science of pure thought, the principle of which is *pure*
> *knowing*, the unity which is not abstract but a living, concrete unity
> in virtue of the fact that in it the opposition in consciousness between
> a self-determined entity, a subject, and a second such entity, an
> object, is known to be overcome; being is known to be the pure
> Notion in its own self, and the pure Notion to be the true being.
> These, then, are the two *moments* contained in logic.

2 The finite and the infinite

The peculiarly Hegelian identification of logic, metaphysics and philosophy of religion is well exemplified by the theme of the relationship
between the finite and the infinite. At the very outset of his 'Lectures on
the Proofs of the Existence of God' Hegel observes that he has chosen a
subject that is connected with the other set of lectures which I gave on
logic . . . a kind of supplement to that set, inasmuch as it is concerned
only with the particular aspect of the fundamental conceptions of logic'
(p. 155). The finite-infinite relationship is only the most abstract aspect
of 'this wealth of relationship which exists between the human spirit
and God', and 'the logical relation is at the same time also the basis of
the movement of the fullness of content'. Indeed, the tension between
the finite and the infinite is at the very heart of Hegel's entire metaphysical enterprise. Emil Fackenheim has expressed this admirably (*op.*
cit., pp. 72-3):

> Hegel has not forgotten that the time which he sees as ripe for
> 'science' is also (like all time) — one of conflict, chance, and brute
> fact, and that he — the self rising to absolute thought — is also a con-
> tingent self in the midst of time. Many years after the composition
> of the *Phenomenology* Hegel wrote: 'I raise myself in thought to the
> Absolute . . . thus being infinite consciousness; yet at the same time

I am finite consciousness . . . . Both aspects seek each other and flee each other . . . I am the struggle between them.' This struggle — and the struggle to resolve the struggle — is in the end the sole theme of the *Phenomenology* and, indeed, of the whole Hegelian philosophy.

The purely logical aspect of the finite-infinite relationship is described thus in *The Science of Logic* (p. 138):

The Notion of the infinite as it first presents itself is this, that determinate being in its being-in-itself determines itself as finite and transcends the limitation. It is the very nature of the finite to transcend itself, to negate its negation and to become infinite. Thus the infinite does not stand as something finished and complete above or superior to the finite, as if the finite had an enduring being *apart from* or *subordinate to* the infinite.

The transition to the 'principles of theology' in the *Encyclopaedia Logic* is noteworthy (p. 103):

And what men call the proofs of God's existence are, rightly understood, ways of describing and analysing the native course of the mind, the course of *thought* thinking the *data* of the senses. The rise of thought beyond the world of sense, its passage from the finite to the infinite, the leap into the super-sensible which it takes when it snaps asunder the chain of sense, all this transition is thought and nothing but thought.

The finite-infinite relationship recurs again in the 'Lectures on the Proofs of the Existence of God'. Thus, apropos the cosmological proof, Hegel writes (p. 348):

Finite Being does not continue to be an Other; there is no gulf between the Infinite and the finite. The finite is something that cancels itself, loses itself in something higher, so that its truth is the Infinite, what has Being in-and-for-itself.

In relation to the teleological proof (p. 352):

The finitude of finite minds is no true Being; it is by its very nature dialectic, which implies that it abrogates itself, negates itself, and the negation of this finitude is affirmation as infinitude, as something universal in-and-for-itself. This is the highest form of the transition; for the transition is here Spirit itself.

The logical concept of the Notion, the finite-infinite relationship, the epistemological (and metaphysical) thesis of the unity of thought and being and the theological idea of the existence of god all cohere in a uniquely Hegelian manner in the following remarkable statement near the end of the 'Lectures on the Proofs of the Existence of God' (p. 362):

> In the case of the finite, existence does not correspond to the Notion. On the other hand, in the case of the Infinite, which is determined within itself, the reality must correspond to the Notion; this is the Ideal, the unity of subject and object.

Chapter 3

Science

3.1

We shall now proceed to an examination of Iqbal's ambitious endeavour to 'examine and interpret experience, following the clue furnished by the Quran which regards experience within and without as symbolic of a reality described by it, as "the First and the Last, the visible and the invisible".' In this way he will attempt to exhibit the true significance of the ontological and the teleological arguments by showing that his 'examination and interpretation' of 'experience' yield the conclusion of the unity of thought and being. Iqbal is endeavouring to arrive at an Hegelian destination by proceeding along, as we shall see, a distinctly *un*-Hegelian route. Be that as it may, it is important to keep his ultimate goal clearly in view as we go on to scrutinise the structure of his elaborate argument.

Iqbal begins: 'Now experience, as unfolding itself in time, presents three main levels – the level of matter, the level of life, and the level of mind and consciousness – the subject matter of physics, biology and psychology, respectively' (p. 31). There is something very peculiar, to say the least, about the notion of 'experience, as unfolding itself in time'. There are hidden assumptions at work – in fact, there is virtually a metaphysic of time: time as an absolute framework within which 'experience' unfolds itself.[1] And what is Iqbal's concept of 'experience'? To judge from the idea that experience 'presents three main levels', etc., it is at least an unexamined notion.[2]

3.2

Iqbal turns first to a consideration of modern physics. A brief characterisation of physics is followed by a discussion of the concept of matter:

18

'In order exactly to appreciate the position of modern physics it is necessary to understand clearly what we mean by matter.' The 'traditional' theory of matter[3] is stated as follows (pp. 32-3):[4]

> The sense objects (colours, sounds, etc.) are states of the perceiver's mind, and as such excluded from nature regarded as something objective. For this reason they cannot be in any proper sense qualities of physical things. When I say the sky is blue, it can only mean that the sky produces a blue sensation in my mind, and not that the colour blue is a quality found in the sky. As mental states they are impressions, that is to say, they are effects produced in us. The cause of these effects is matter, or material things acting through our sense organs, nerves and brain on our mind. This physical cause acts by contact or impact; hence it must possess the qualities of shape, size, solidity and resistance.

Whitehead's critique, or at least the gist of some of its main arguments, is next presented. The central one, as stated by Iqbal, is that (p. 33):

> if physics constitutes a really coherent and genuine knowledge of perceptively known objects, the traditional theory of matter must be rejected for the obvious reason that it reduces the evidence of our senses, on which alone the physicist, as observer and experimenter, must rely, to the mere impressions of the observer's mind.

As thus stated, the exposition does great injustice to the detailed and complex nature of Whitehead's own argumentation, for instance in *The Concept of Nature* (1920) and *Science and the Modern World* (1925). (Both these works, as well as the earlier *The Principles of Natural Knowledge* (1919), were available at the time when Iqbal was writing.'

Einstein fares worse. The assertion that 'the concept of matter has received the greatest blow from the hand of Einstein' is merely backed up by a single, all too brief, quotation from Russell (p. 34):[5]

> The theory of Relativity by merging time into space-time has damaged the traditional notion of substance more than all the arguments of the philosophers. Matter, for commonsense, is something which persists in time and moves in space. But for modern relativity-physics this view is no longer tenable. A piece of matter has become not a persistent thing with varying states, but a system of inter-related events. The old solidity is gone, and with it the characteristics that to the materialist made matter seem more real than fleeting thoughts.

The crucial distinction between a scientific notion and its possible philosophical implications is not made. In consequence, the interpretative nature of Russell's position is not recognised. In fact it is arguable that Russell's statement, unless carefully qualified, is quite misleading. It is not even clear whether 'matter' is being considered in the cosmological perspective, i.e., within the Einsteinian space-time framework, or in the micro-physical perspective.

The discussion of this issue in Russell's *ABC of Relativity* would appear to involve a similar confusion of scientific and philosophical notions of 'matter' and 'substance'. In general it is probably safe to say that Einstein's theory does not have any significant *philosophical* consequences for the concept of matter.[6]

Iqbal's treatment of Whitehead (and Einstein) is superficial in the extreme and it is therefore not surprising to find him drawing some extravagant conclusions from it. Consider for instance:

(1) In our own times Professor Whitehead – an eminent mathematician and scientist – has conclusively shown that the traditional theory of materialism is wholly untenable (p. 33).
(2) Thus physics, finding it necessary to criticise its own foundations, has eventually found reason to break its own idol, and the empirical attitude which appeared to necessitate scientific materialism has finally ended in a revolt against matter (p. 33).

Whitehead's argument (*The Concept of Nature*) is sustained and persuasive but it is directed at theories of the bifurcation of nature, and there is no question of a categorical refutation of 'the traditional theory of materialism', as claimed by Iqbal. Whitehead writes: (p. 30)

What I am essentially protesting against is the bifurcation of nature into two systems of reality, which, in so far as they are real, are real in different senses. One reality would be the entities such as electrons which are the objects of study of speculative physics. This would be the reality which is there for knowledge; although on this theory it is never known. For what is known is the other sort of reality, which is the byplay of the mind. Thus there would be two natures, one is the conjecture and the other is the dream.

In any case 'its own idol' is not necessarily 'scientific materialism' and it is quite misleading to speak of the scientific attitude as having 'finally ended in a revolt against matter'. Iqbal does not see the important distinction between a scientific idea and its philosophical interpretation. Thus 'matter', as conceived and studied by science, and 'materialism' (or even 'scientific materialism') are two very different things – the former is a *scientific* concept whereas the latter term denotes a particular metaphysical position, i.e., it is a *philosophical* concept. Whitehead's declared aim is 'To lay the basis of a natural philosophy which is the necessary pre-supposition of a reorganised speculative physics.' And again: 'The primary task of a philosophy of natural science is to elucidate the concept of nature' (*The Concept of Nature*, pp. vii, 46). Iqbal goes on (p. 34):

> According to Professor Whitehead, therefore, Nature is not a static fact situated in a dynamic void, but a structure of events possessing the character of a continuous creative flow which thought cuts up into isolated immobilities out of whose mutual relations arise the concepts of space and time.

But this concept of nature does not follow from what Iqbal has just stated about Whitehead. Indeed, we must go further – the notion of nature as 'a structure of events possessing the character of a continuous creative flow' is a bare schematic formula and does not render intelligible the total metaphysical vision it is, presumably, supposed to represent. In order to render it intelligible we would have to expound the main principles of the Whiteheadian philosophy – perhaps beginning thus (*The Concept of Nature*, p. 52):

> What we discern is the specific character of a place through a period of time. This is what I mean by an 'event'. We discern some specific character of an event. But in discerning an event we are also aware of its significance as a relatum in the structure of events. This structure of events is the complex of events as related by the two relations of extension and cogredience. The most simple expression of the properties of this structure are to be found in our spatial and temporal relations. A discerned event is known as related in this structure to other events whose specific characters are otherwise not disclosed in that immediate awareness except so far as that they are relata within the structure.

3.3

Immediately after introducing the subject of space Iqbal launches into an irrelevant excursus on Zeno's paradoxes. The two well-known arguments against motion (the Race Course and the Arrow) are considered and the views of Bergson and Russell discussed. Even the tradition of Muslim thought (Al-Ashari, d. 935, Ibn Hazm, d. 1064) is brought to bear on these issues. All this in the minute compass of two and a half pages. Iqbal takes the view that 'The ancient Greek philosopher Zeno approached the problem of space through the question of movement in space', so that he is able to conclude that 'The unreality of movement means the unreality of an independent space'. I will not enter into these questions here since, as already stated, I incline to the position that Zeno is not relevant to a discussion of the subject of space in modern physics. His two arguments are directed against the idea of motion (see G. Vlastos, 'Zeno of Elea', *Encyclopaedia of Philosophy*, 1967, vol. 8). Essentially it is part of 'the defence of the *logos* of Parmenides' – namely, that reality is one, indivisible, motionless (W. K. C. Guthrie, *History of Greek Philosophy*, 1969, vol. II, p. 100). However, it may be arguable that they provide an indirect way of entering into the problem of space. Thus, Grünbaum is of the opinion that (*Modern Science and Zeno's Paradoxes*, 1968, p. 3):

> These were designed to show that the science of geometry is beset by a paradox and that any attempt to provide a mathematical description of motion becomes ensnared in contradictions. So seminal was the scientific challenge bequeathed to posterity by Zeno's polemic that the contemporary philosopher Bertrand Russell paid tribute to him, saying 'Zeno's arguments, in some form, have afforded grounds for almost all the theories of space and time and infinity which have been constructed from his day to our own'.

3.4

We return to Iqbal's consideration of the problem of space. He introduces the problem thus: 'The scientific view of nature as pure materiality is associated with the Newtonian view of space as an absolute void in which things are situated' (p. 34). Inevitably Einstein is brought into the discussion, which is tantalisingly brief and sketchy. Reference is made to 'Einstein's Theory' and 'Einstein's Relativity' but no distinction is made between the general and the special theories of relativity. A presentation which is so superficial and disjointed cannot but be misleading. (Indeed, it cannot even warrant detailed examination here.) The minute scale of his exposition does not, however, deter Iqbal from making the bold metaphysical declamation that (p. 38):

> Personally, I believe that the ultimate character of Reality is spiritual: but in order to avoid a widespread misunderstanding it is necessary to point out that Einstein's Theory of Relativity, which as a scientific

theory deals only with the structure of things, throws no light on the ultimate nature of things which possess that structure.

How is this dichotomy — the structure of things/the ultimate nature of things which possess that structure — arrived at? It has often been argued with force and persuasion, and not only by positivists or materialists, that science *does* deal with 'the ultimate nature of things'.[7]

Iqbal's statements about 'the philosophical value of the theory' (e.g., 'First, it destroys, not the objectivity of Nature, but the view of substance as simple location in space — a view which led to materialism in Classical Physics') are clearly of Whiteheadian derivation. However, Iqbal is here confusing scientific and philosophical ideas: instead of the 'matter' of physics he writes of 'substance', which is a metaphysical notion. Again, 'materialism' is a philosophical idea and there is no necessary, or straightforward, connection or transition between the 'matter' of physics and 'materialism'. Again, he errs when he writes that 'In Whitehead's presentation of the theory the notion of "matter" is entirely replaced by the notion of "organism".' Whitehead's concept of organism is in fact fundamental to his whole metaphysic, but in itself it (the concept of organism) has nothing to do with Einstein's theory of relativity. Thus Whitehead (*Science and the Modern World*) states quite explicitly (p. 121):

What we must now ask of philosophy is to give us an interpretation of the status in nature of space and time, so that the possibility of alternative meanings is preserved . . . I am pre-supposing the organic theory of nature, which I have outlined as the basis for a thoroughgoing objectivism.

And again: 'In an organic philosophy of nature there is nothing to decide between the old hypothesis of the uniqueness of the time discrimination and the new hypothesis of its multiplicity. It is purely a matter for evidence drawn from observations' (ch. VII, p. 123). In other words Whitehead is saying quite plainly that his basic premise is the metaphysical one of the organic theory of nature. Now on this basis he conceives the further task of philosophy to be that of providing *alternative* interpretations of the scientific concepts of space and time. Further, while allowing that the actual empirical data must come from scientific observations Whitehead is arguing that his theory of nature as organism is compatible with both, the older (Newtonian) notion of the uniqueness of simultaneity, as well as the modern (Einsteinian) one of its relativity. It is therefore quite wrong to say, as Iqbal does, that it is in Whitehead's presentation of Einstein's theory that the notion of

23

organism replaces that of matter. After all, 'Philosophy is not one among the sciences with its own little scheme of abstractions which it works away at perfecting and improving. It is the survey of the sciences, with the special objects of their harmony, and of their completion' (*Science and the Modern World*, ch. 5, p. 88).

Iqbal goes on to assert that Einstein's theory 'presents one great difficulty, i.e., the unreality of time . . . time as a free creative movement has no meaning for the theory.' At this point a major inconsistency appears: 'Nor is it possible for us laymen to understand what is the real nature of Einstein's time.' Despite this admission Iqbal proceeds, without compunction, to the further contradictory assertion — 'It is obvious that Einstein's time is not Bergson's pure duration. Nor can we regard it as serial time. Serial time is the essence of causality as defined by Kant.'

So far from implying 'the unreality of time' Einstein takes time very seriously — indeed, it has a fundamental importance as the fourth coordinate in his four-dimensional space-time continuum. It is only thus that we can arrive at the notion of 'the peculiar geometrical configuration of space-time'.[8] Although time is subjected to such a sophisticated and abstract geometrical treatment, it is none the less important to see that Einstein's time is the time of our ordinary common-sense experience and knowledge.

We have found Iqbal's discussion of modern physics and related philosophical issues inadequate. This applies particularly both to his treatment of Whitehead and to his exposition of Einstein's theory of relativity. It is also significant that he does not draw any conclusion of either a general or a specific nature at this stage.

3.5

In the next section, Iqbal discusses the problems of life and consciousness. It begins with a statement about the nature of consciousness, which appears to be based on William James. (Particularly suggestive of the Jamesian influence is the following: 'It has no well-defined *fringes*; it shrinks and expands as the occasion demands.' My emphasis.) The problem of mechanistic or causal *versus* teleological explanation in biology is prefaced by a general reflection on the nature of natural science: 'The question, then, is whether the passage to Reality through the revelations of sense-perception necessarily leads to a view of Reality essentially opposed to the view that religion takes of its ultimate character' (p. 41). Iqbal's answer is that the various sciences of nature inevitably study nature piecemeal — 'Science is not a single systematic view of Reality. It is a mass of sectional views of Reality.' But when nature is seen within the totality of human experience an altogether new perspective is revealed. 'Thus religion, which demands the whole of Reality and for this reason must occupy a central place in any synthesis of all the data of human experience, has no reason to be afraid of any sectional views of Reality' (p. 42). The thesis of the inadequacy of a mechanistic explanation of biological phenomena is then defended mainly by invoking the authority of J. S. Haldane and Wildon Carr.

3.6

Some general remarks on the relationship between science and philosophy would be in order. The contact, or at times interaction, between these two disciplines has had a chequered history throughout the western intellectual tradition. At the present time two principal, but not necessarily mutually exclusive, areas of contact are discernible. First, there is 'philosophy of science' as the specific discipline dealing with the problems and methodology of science. Second, there are the various approaches designed to incorporate scientific findings within a more or less comprehensive philosophical world-view; for instance, the Whiteheadian cosmology belongs to this category. As more recent and noteworthy examples of the latter type of endeavour we may mention the outstanding, but widely ignored, contributions of Errol E. Harris (especially his *Foundations of Metaphysics in Science*) and Hans Jonas (*The Phenomenon of Life*). Iqbal's discussion of science remains as a half-way house — an unsatisfactory attempt to expound some important scientific ideas largely in terms of their philosophical implications. To the extent that he is developing, or presenting, a metaphysic he is quite unoriginal; in the main he simply follows Whitehead and Bergson.

Chapter 4

Bergson

4.1

Iqbal's exposition and critique of the Bergsonian philosophy is prefaced by the statement that he will 'try to reach the primacy of life and thought by another route'. This is also expected to reveal 'the nature of life as a psychic activity'. There is then an attempt to relate the Whiteheadian idea of the passage of nature to the Quran.[1]

Iqbal's discussion of Bergson is the fullest accorded to any single thinker in his work – amounting to almost one-third of the entire chapter we are dealing with. (The texts are probably, *Time and Free Will*, *Creative Evolution* and *Introduction to Metaphysics*.)

I shall present Iqbal's own case in outline and then comment on it. Iqbal begins (p. 46):

> Among the representatives of contemporary thought Bergson is the only thinker who has made a keen study of the phenomenon of duration in time. I will first briefly explain to you his view of duration and then point out the inadequacy of his analysis in order fully to bring out the implications of a completer view of the temporal aspect of existence. The Ontological problem before us is how to define the ultimate nature of existence.

Since the existence (in time) of the external world is not indubitable we must find a privileged case of existence which cannot be doubted and, further, which also affords a direct experience of the (Bergsonian) phenomenon of time duration. Such a privileged case is found in my perception of my own self, which is 'internal, intimate, and profound' as contrasted with my perception of things in the outside world, which is 'superficial and external'. 'It follows, therefore, that conscious experience is that privileged case of existence in which we are in absolute contact with Reality, and an analysis of this privileged case is likely to throw a flood of light on the ultimate meaning of existence' (p. 46).

When I inspect the conscious experience of my own inner life I find nothing static — 'All is a constant mobility, an unceasing flux of states, a perpetual flow in which there is no halt or resting place.' Such change is unthinkable without time; conscious existence is therefore life in time. A further analysis of our conscious experience reveals that the self has two aspects — efficient and appreciative. The efficient self is the ordinary subject of daily life which enters into relation with the spatial world. This self lives outside itself and 'discloses itself as nothing more than a series of specific and consequently numerable states. The time in which the efficient self lives is therefore the time of which we predicate long and short. It is hardly distinguishable from space' (p. 47). It can be conceived spatially as a straight line — but, according to Bergson, this spatialised time is not true time. True time is the time of the appreciative self which is revealed by a deeper view of conscious experience. It is extremely difficult to see the appreciative self since the veil woven around it by our absorption in external things is lifted 'only in the moments of profound meditation when the efficient self is in abeyance'. The states of consciousness of this deeper ego (the appreciative self) inter-penetrate to form an indivisible unity so that its time 'is a single "now" . . . pure duration unadulterated by space'. (The efficient self in its traffic with the spatial world pulverises this single 'now' into a series of 'nows'.) This inner experience of pure duration cannot be expressed in words since language is based on the serial time of the efficient self.

Within the organic wholeness of pure time the past operates in the present, and the future is also present in it as an open possibility. Creative activity, as opposed to mechanical and repetitive activity, is free and therefore the creative activity of life cannot be explained on a mechanistic basis. Science tries to establish 'the laws of mechanical repetition', but the spontaneous activity of life is outside the sphere of necessity. 'Hence science cannot comprehend life.' The universe is a creative and continuous movement, but thought, according to Bergson, works in a serial fashion with static concepts. In this way the dynamic act which is the universe is reduced by the operation of thought to a series of stationary points — thus yielding our ideas of space and time. 'According to Bergson, then, Reality is a free unpredictable, creative, vital impetus of the nature of volition which thought spatialises and views as a plurality of "things" ' (p. 51).

4.2

Iqbal's critique follows his exposition; three main points are made.

(1) Bergson's vitalism 'ends in an insurmountable dualism of will and thought'. Iqbal attributes this dualism to Bergson's inadequate grasp of the nature of the intellect, and then tries to resolve it by invoking the idea of the deeper movement of thought which he has already adumbrated (see p. 5, no. 2).

(2) Iqbal's chief criticism is that 'In Bergson's view the forward rush of the vital impulse in its creative freedom is unilluminated by the light of an immediate or remote purpose' (p. 52). Bergson 'denies the Teleological character of Reality on the ground that Teleology makes time unreal' (p. 53). Iqbal's own view is that human life shows a teleological development in the sense that 'while there is no far-off distant goal towards which we are moving, there is a progressive formation of fresh ends, purposes, and ideal scales of value' (p. 54).

(3) 'I venture to think that the error of Bergson consists in regarding pure time as prior to self, to which alone pure duration is predicable' (p. 55).

4.3 Comments on Iqbal's exposition and critique of Bergson

Iqbal is not faithful to Bergson and his account is misleading in several respects. These are the result of a wrong reading of Bergson. My summary of his exposition aims at clarity and succinctness and this tends to mask many of Iqbal's erroneous interpretations. Consider some examples.

(a) 'The Ontological problem before us is how to define the ultimate nature of existence' (p. 46). Bergson does not pose the problem in terms of such traditional metaphysical categories.

(b) 'Existence in spatialised time is spurious existence' (p. 47). It is spatialised time, and not existence, which is spurious.

(c) Iqbal's exasperatingly varied use of the word 'reality'. Take Bergson's own statements. The 'consciousness we have of our own self in its continual flux introduces us to the interior of a reality, on the model of which we must represent other realities' (pp. 49-50). 'This intuition attains the absolute' (*Introduction to Metaphysics*, p. 53). What is this 'reality' attained as 'the absolute' in Bergsonian intuition? Bergson is quite explicit − 'our Reality seen from within by intuition is our self which endures'. Again, 'an inner, absolute knowledge of the duration of the self by the self is possible' (*Introduction to Metaphysics* p. 31).

This simple schema is later complicated by the introduction of the notion of the vital impetus (which is also intuitable). The vital impetus is subsequently regarded as a 'supra-consciousness' which is called 'God' in *Creative Evolution* (see T. A. Goudge, 'Bergson', *Encyclopaedia of Philosophy*, vol. 1). Such a development clearly raises more problems than it solves. How, for instance, does 'intuition' distinguish between the inner reality of the self and the vital impetus? And so on. To return to Iqbal, we have already seen that according to Iqbal Bergsonian intuition reveals 'that privileged case of existence in which we are in absolute contact with Reality'. Thus stated, 'reality' is whatever is found inside. But in the next few pages Iqbal uses the word 'reality' in at least three further senses: (1) God (on p. 50 'reality' is equated with the Quranic god). (2) The whole evolutionary process, e.g., pp. 51, 53. (3) The whole order of nature or the totality of the external world, e.g., p. 52. These distinctions are quite plain even though they are not explicitly articulated by Iqbal.

(d) Consider the concluding statement in Iqbal's exposition: 'According to Bergson, then, Reality is a free unpredictable, creative, vital impetus of the nature of volition which thought spatialises and views as a plurality of "things" ' (p. 51). What is "Reality"? Presumably the entire process of biological evolution. But then this is equated with the vital impetus and this is most un-Bergsonian.

4.4

Take Iqbal's criticisms in order.

(1) The charge that Bergsonian vitalism 'ends in an insurmountable dualism of will and thought'. It is not clear to what the word 'will' refers. There is of course in Bergson the obvious, and indeed even outstanding, dualism of intellect and intuition. Iqbal substitutes 'intelligence' for 'thought', and the two terms are then used interchangeably. Similarly 'will' becomes 'life'. So Iqbal eventually argues for the unity of 'life and thought' and further asserts that thought, 'in its true nature, is identical with life'. The 'deeper movement of thought' upon which Iqbal tries to base his argument is itself a Bergsonian-Hegelian hybrid. It is here developed along the lines that the function of thought is 'to synthesise the elements of experience . . . it is as much organic as life . . . it is determined by ends . . . and permeated by intelligence.' Now this is very different from, and indeed arguably inconsistent with, his own earlier formulation (*The Reconstruction*, pp. 5-7) — to which he is ostensibly

appealing — which begins with Bergsonian-sounding references (to 'thought and intuition', 'serial time' and the like), but subsequently progresses in an overtly Hegelian manner (thought reaches 'an immanent Infinite in whose self-unfolding movement the various finite concepts are merely moments'). What is more serious is that this notion of thought (as teleology) is also widely divergent from what it is, presumably, supposed to be — the Bergsonian concept of the intellect (as practical activity). But even if we wish, as a last resort, to give Iqbal the benefit of the doubt and grant that he is in effect, at least in plan and purpose, grappling with the problems posed by the Bergsonian dualism of intellect and intuition his case has not been made out. He has taken liberties in changing his terminology abruptly and without warning — and indeed, in a manner which seems almost calculated to provoke charges of arbitrariness. There are wholesale distortions of Bergson. Further, Iqbal's argumentation is inconsistent as well as confused. In a word, it is a philosophical farrago.

(2) Consider next Iqbal's principal complaint against Bergson — that he 'denies the Teleological character of Reality on the ground that Teleology makes time unreal'. In fact two distinct spheres are implicated in this discussion: individual human life and biological evolution. The first question is obviously what we are to understand by the term 'teleology'. In its current (modern) usage the term simply means goal-directed behaviour, and it is applicable both to living and non-living systems (see Beckner, 1967). In the realm of life a further distinction must be made between the goal-directed behaviour of consciously purposing human agents and the relatively simpler type of teleological behaviour shown by organisms lower down the evolutionary scale. Further, there is the question of the goal-directedness of the whole process of biological evolution.[2] We must next examine Bergson's and Iqbal's uses of this term.

In *Creative Evolution* Bergson uses the term 'finalism', and this is equated with 'teleology'. Thus his case against radical mechanism (*sic*) is followed by that against radical finalism (p. 41).

> But radical finalism is quite as unacceptable, and for the same reason. The doctrine of Teleology, in its extreme form, as we find it in Leibniz for example, implies that things and beings merely realise the programme previously arranged . . . time is useless again. As in the mechanistic hypothesis, here again it is supposed that, *all is given.* Finalism thus understood is only inverted mechanism.

Bergson goes on to argue that unlike mechanism the doctrine of finalism is not fixed and rigid. So much so that 'it admits of as many inflections as we like'. So that 'its principle, which is essentially psychological, is very flexible. It is so extensible, and thereby so comprehensive, that one accepts something of it as soon as one rejects pure mechanism.' Therefore the doctrine of final causes can never be definitively refuted; and, indeed, 'the theory which I will put forward in this book will therefore necessarily partake of finalism to a certain extent'. This plain statement of Bergson's should serve as a warning against any attempt at a simple blanket criticism such as the charge that Bergson denies teleology. Clearly, Iqbal has not heeded this warning.

The essence of Iqbal's criticism hinges around the related notions of ends, purposes and values; and his insistence that such notions are implicated in Bergson's rejection of teleology. He agrees with Bergson in the denial of teleology in the sense that approximates to the Aristotelian doctrine of final causes, *viz.* 'the working out of a plan in view of a predetermined end or goal' (*The Reconstruction*, p. 54). This view, argues Iqbal, makes time unreal since the universe is reduced 'to a mere temporal reproduction of a pre-existing eternal scheme or structure'. No scope is left for human freedom, so it cannot be a world of 'free, responsible moral agents'. At this point Iqbal suggests another sense of teleology — individual human lives involve 'a progressive formation of fresh ends, purposes, and ideal scales of value'. But in his anxiety to keep out his first, rejected, sense of teleology he makes it quite plain that 'there is no far-off distant goal towards which we are moving'. His anxiety is misplaced since *logically* there is no difference between a goal that is near at hand and one that is distant. (Thus a distant goal turns out to be a necessary but not sufficient condition of teleology in the first sense.) We must now see if Iqbal is right in maintaining that Bergson denies teleology in the second sense as well.

We have already noted Bergson's admission that some form of teleology (finalism) is essential to his own theory (*Creative Evolution*). This is in fact already clear from his earlier discussion in *Time and Free Will* (1910). There, the ideas of deliberation and choice are central to his whole case against determinism. If human beings are consciously reflecting agents who can deliberate and make particular choices then clearly this is perfectly compatible with the choice of specific goals, purposes and values. Indeed, it could even be argued that the latter are, in some sense, logically implied by the former. This argument is considerably strengthened by a consideration of Bergson's development of the idea of finalism in *Creative Evolution*. Take the following statements: 'we think only in order to act . . . now, in order to act, we begin by proposing an end; we make a plan'; 'And it may equally well be said that each action is the realisation of an intention'. Bergson emphasises that although he wants to go beyond both mechanism and finalism his position lies nearer the latter doctrine. 'Like radical finalism, although in a vaguer form, our philosophy represents the organised world as a harmonious whole.' He is most explicit in the concluding section ('Result of the Enquiry — The Vital Impetus') of chapter 1 of *Creative Evolution* (p. 102). Life involves action 'But this action always presents, to some extent, the character of contingency; it implies at least a rudiment of choice. Now choice involves the anticipatory idea of several possible actions. Possibilities of action must therefore be marked out for the living being before the action itself.'[3] Thus there are no grounds whatsoever for Iqbal's criticism of Bergson on this particular score.

(3) This is a monumental error on Iqbal's part. It is as clear as the light of day that the notion of 'pure time as prior to self' is totally self-contradictory (i.e., the *Bergsonian* idea of pure time or real duration).

4.5 General comments on Iqbal's assessment of Bergson

Iqbal has not made an incisive or substantial criticism of any of Bergson's major doctrines. Indeed, whatever he offers by way of assessment and critical appraisal is confused, timid and ineffectual — or simply erroneous. This contrasts sharply with the critiques developed, for instance, by Russell, Merleau-Ponty and Collingwood; these philosophers have made impressive criticisms of a central and decisive kind. Especially noteworthy is Collingwood's assessment — admirable in its combination of balance, concision, clear-headedness and cogency. Thus he allows that 'The high and permanent merit of Bergson's theory of nature is that he is in earnest with the conception of life; he has grasped that conception with great firmness and defined it in a way which is not only brilliant and impressive but within its own limits conclusive' (*The Idea of Nature*, p. 138). Nevertheless there are serious weaknesses which demand analysis — such as the dualism of matter and life. Collingwood argues that Bergson has to fall back stepwise on two further dualisms — the first between intellect and intuition, and the second between knowledge and action. Of these three dualisms 'the one which is fundamental for our purpose is the cosmological dualism between matter and life' (p. 139). He goes on to argue that Bergson is unable to resolve it and that 'the position he is defending is a monstrous and intolerable paradox' (p. 139). Further scrutiny of Bergson's fundamental concept of the vital impetus ('the life-force' in Collingwood's terms) reveals the vicious circle of his cosmology. 'This conclusion is fatal to Bergson's theory of knowledge' (p. 140). Eventually Bergson is left 'in the dilemma of either tacitly asserting what he professes to deny or else asserting nothing except the existence of force which does nothing and of an intuition that apprehends that nothingness' (p. 141). 'What is wrong with Bergson's philosophy, regarded as a cosmology, is not the fact that he takes life seriously but the fact that he takes nothing else seriously' (p. 141).

A direct consequence of this lack of deep criticism on Iqbal's part is the fact that he has swallowed Bergson's fundamental doctrine of time as 'pure duration' hook, line and sinker. This applies particularly to its metaphysical trappings; but this is only the beginning of the story. Uncritical acceptance of such Bergsonian notions as pure duration, the two selves (appreciative and efficient), and the internal reality which is intuitible, leads Iqbal on, almost insensibly, to an illegitimate extension of their meaning and implications. Thus Iqbal is driven inexorably on to such dogmatic assertions as 'Conscious experience is that privileged case of existence in which we are in absolute contact with Reality'; time is 'An essential element of the ultimate Reality' since 'The ultimate Reality' is conceived as 'Pure duration in which thought, life, and purpose interpenetrate to form an organic unity'. Such strong claims are certainly not warranted by anything in Bergson's writings.[4] The position does not improve when we inspect Iqbal's own case — there is simply no independent argumentation. Even in such an immediately relevant Bergsonian text as *An Introduction to Metaphysics* the metaphysical principles that are spelled out seem provisional rather than absolutely assured; they lack the firmness and solidity which would be needed if the entire structure was to bear the metaphysical load that Iqbal, perhaps unwittingly, puts on it. When we go on presently to consider Iqbal's concept of god and nature we shall find that the Bergsonian influence has been decisive.

Chapter 5

Conclusions and critique

(A) Iqbal's Conclusions: God and Nature

5.1

In the final section of this part (chapter 2 of *The Reconstruction*) Iqbal draws his conclusions and states the major theses of his position – as the culmination, he believes, of the elaborate philosophical inquiry which precedes it. Our next task, therefore, must be a statement of these conclusions and theses.

We are now in a position to understand the Quranic verse, 'And it is He Who hath ordained the night and day to succeed one another for those who desire to think on God or desire to be thankful' (25.62). 'A critical interpretation of the sequence of time as revealed in ourselves has led us to a notion of the ultimate Reality as pure duration in which thought, life, and purposes inter-penetrate to form an organic unity' (p. 55). This unity is only conceivable as the unity of 'an all-embracing concrete self – the ultimate source of all individual life and thought.'

Pure time is only predicable as the appreciative act of an enduring self (p. 56):

> To exist in pure duration is to be a self, and to be a self is to be able to say 'I am'. Only that truly exists which can say 'I am'. It is the degree of the intuition of 'I-amness' that determines the place of a thing in the scale of being.

We, as human beings, do say 'I am' but this is dependent on the distinction of self and not-self. The ultimate self in the Quranic phrase, 'can afford to dispense with all the worlds'. The ultimate self, unlike the finite human self, is not confronted by a not-self as an 'other' which

34

stands in an external (spatial) relationship to it. 'What we call Nature or the not-self is only a fleeting moment in the life of God. His "I-amness" is independent, elemental, absolute. Of such a self it is impossible for us to form an adequate conception. As the Quran says, "Naught is like Him; yet He hears and sees" '

We have already seen that nature is a structure of events (pp. 56-7):

a systematic mode of behaviour, and as such organic to the ultimate Self. Nature is to the Divine Self as character is to the human self. In the picturesque phrase of the Quran it is the habit of Allah. From the human point of view it is an interpretation which, in our present situation, we put on the creative activity of the Absolute Ego. At a particular moment in its forward movement it is finite; but since the self to which it is organic is creative, it is liable to increase, and is consequently boundless in the sense that no limit to its extension is final. Its boundlessness is potential, not actual. Nature, then, must be understood as a living, ever-growing organism whose growth has no final external limits. Its only limit is internal, i.e., the immanent self which animates and sustains the whole. As the Quran says: 'And verily unto thy Lord is the limit' (53:42). Thus the view that we have taken gives a fresh spiritual meaning to physical science. The knowledge of Nature is the knowledge of God's behaviour. In our observation of Nature we are virtually seeking a kind of intimacy with the Absolute Ego; and this is only another form of worship.

In these statements time is taken 'as an essential element of the ultimate Reality'. McTaggart's argument about the unreality of time concerns itself only with serial time, to which the 'past, present, and future' schema applies. Real time, however, is pure duration and this remains entirely unaffected by McTaggart's argument. 'Serial time is pure duration pulverised by thought — a kind of device by which Reality exposes its ceaseless creative activity to quantitative measurement' (p. 58). This reveals the meaning of the Quranic verse, 'And of Him is the change of the night and of the day.'

5.2

But the important question is, 'Can change be predicated of the Ultimate Ego?' Human life is conditioned by many external factors and change and imperfection are necessary ingredients in it. (In fact 'change is essentially imperfection'.) Since 'our conscious experience is the only point of departure for all knowledge' certain limitations are necessarily imposed on our thinking. Thus when we think of god we tend to anthropomorphize. This led the Spanish Muslim theologian Ibn Hazm to make the ingenious suggestion that god should be regarded as living, not in the human sense, but only because he is so described in the Quran. Ibn Hazm was probably dealing only with serial change – an obvious mark of imperfection; hence he could not reconcile divine perfection with divine life. This problem may be resolved as follows. 'The Absolute Ego, as we have seen, is the whole of Reality . . . the phases of His life are wholly determined from within' (p. 59). Serial change is not applicable to his life. 'The Ultimate Ego exists in pure duration wherein change ceases to be a succession of varying attitudes, and reveals its true character as continuous creation, "untouched by weariness" and unseizable "by slumber or sleep".' 'The perfection of the Creative Self . . . consists in the vaster basis of His creative activity and the infinite scope of His creative vision. God's life is self-revelation, not the pursuit of an ideal to be reached' (p. 60).

5.3

Thus a comprehensive philosophical criticism of all the facts of experience on its efficient as well as appreciative side brings us to the conclusion that the ultimate Reality is a rationally directed creative life. To interpret this life as an ego is not to fashion God after the image of man. It is only to accept the simple fact of experience that life is not a formless fluid, but an organizing principle of unity (p. 60).

'*The result of an intellectual view of life, therefore, is necessarily pantheistic*' (my italics). But appreciative intuition (of which 'we have a first-hand knowledge . . . from within') 'Reveals life as a centralizing ego'. This knowledge constitutes 'a direct revelation of the ultimate nature of Reality. Thus the facts of experience justify the inference that the ultimate nature of Reality is spiritual, and must be conceived as an ego' (p. 61).

(B) Overall Critique

5.4

Iqbal commenced with a discussion of the cosmological, teleological and ontological proofs of the existence of god. He found them logically inadequate. To recapitulate. The cosmological argument makes an illegitimate move – from finite to infinite by merely negating or contradicting the finite. Here Iqbal introduces the (Hegelian) notion of 'the true infinite'. The teleological argument fails because it yields a finite external designer – like 'a human mechanician'. It is based on a false analogy between the human artificer or architect and the phenomena of nature. The ontological argument involves a *petitio principii*: the transition from the logical to the real. This is similar to the cosmological argument. Essentially the teleological and the ontological arguments fail because they regard 'thought' as an external agency working on 'things'. Hence they result, in the first case in a 'mere mechanician', and in the second, create an unbridgeable gulf between the ideal and the real. At this stage Iqbal introduced the Hegelian thesis of the unity of thought and being, and argued that 'The true significance of the Ontological and the Teleological arguments will appear only if we are able to show that the human situation is not final and that thought and being are ultimately one.' This led him to assert that such a unity would be demonstrated 'if we carefully examine and interpret experience'. The subsequent extended consideration of the knowledge of nature yielded by the natural sciences was meant to be the implementation of this aim *viz*., the examination and interpretation of 'experience' with the ultimate purpose of showing the unity of thought and being.

5.5

We have already noted the inadequacy of Iqbal's discussions of modern science – principally on the grounds of their excessive brevity and superficiality of treatment, and weak argumentation. We are now led to an even more serious charge – Iqbal has evidently lost sight of the stated goal of his inquiry. It is not clear in what way his discussions of modern science and philosophy are concerned with showing the unity of thought and being. Perhaps the reference to this thesis (of the unity of thought and being) in his discussion of Bergson may serve as an important clue. There he relates this thesis specifically to the alleged Bergsonian 'dualism of will and thought'. But although he refers at this point to his own very Hegelian statement of the thesis of the unity of thought and being in his previous lecture it is quite plain that it has now undergone a radical metamorphosis in an un-Hegelian direction: for now it is the notion of rational, intelligent ends and purposes in life that is held up as an exemplification of the thought-being unity. 'In conscious experience life and thought permeate each other. They form a unity. Thought, therefore, in its true nature, is identical with life.' We can only presume that it is only through some such covert manoeuvre that Iqbal's general conclusions[1] are thought by him to contain an at least implicit demonstration of the unity of thought and being. But this state of affairs is clearly as unsatisfactory as it is un-Hegelian. This is not all. Even if we grant, for the sake of argument, that a case for the thought-being unity has been made out it is, once again, very far from clear in what way this reveals 'The true significance of the Ontological and the Teleological arguments'. The most that can be claimed is that Iqbal has argued for (and we are not now concerned with the cogency of his argument) the spiritual nature of reality – in fact, on his own explicit admission, for some form of pantheism. But he also argues that this reality must be conceived as an ego and this ego is implicitly equated or identified with god. Presumably we are to understand that this is really the deeper significance of the teleological and ontological arguments – namely, the demonstration of the spiritual nature of reality *via* the establishment of the metaphysical doctrine of the unity of thought and being. But then clearly this is too general a goal and no justice is thereby done to the peculiar and specific forms of the teleological and ontological arguments. Indeed, Iqbal does not even as much as mention these arguments either during the course of his 'examination and interpretation of experience' or when he draws his conclusions. This is a lapse and an omission of the most serious kind, and one, indeed, which facilitates the process of critical scrutiny by enabling a judgment to be passed entirely on the basis of his own standards. To sum up, Iqbal has lost sight of the dual goal expressly articulated at the very beginning of his inquiry. More specifically he has failed to show how the metaphysical principle of the unity of thought and being reveals the true significance of the teleological and ontological arguments. In fact, the unity of thought and being itself remains over as an assumption which Iqbal has not made good. Therefore we must conclude that his enterprise is internally self-vitiating since he has not succeeded in terms of his own explicitly declared standards and criteria.

(C) Return to Hegel

5.6

We have already noted the heavy Hegelian influence on Iqbal – the evidence for this is as massive as it is obvious. But we have also observed that Iqbal was 'endeavouring to arrive at an Hegelian destination by proceeding along . . . a distinctly un-Hegelian route' (see above, p. 18). We cannot, of course, object to Iqbal's consideration of the facts of nature *simpliciter*, for was Hegel not himself a great philosopher of nature? Indeed, Collingwood has argued that modern science has arrived at a distinctly Hegelian conception of nature, and this is especially clear in the case of the Whiteheadian philosophy (Collingwood *The Idea of Nature*). More recently an argument along these lines has been developed with very considerable skill and force, and in great detail, by Errol E. Harris (*Nature, Mind and Modern Science* and *The Foundations of Metaphysics in Science*). The objection is rather to the suggestion that the unity of thought and being will be demonstrated by a straightforward consideration of scientific knowledge, for this is what Iqbal's enterprise in 'examining and interpreting experience' amounts to.

It does therefore seem pertinent to inquire about the precise nature of the Iqbalian enterprise in the light of the evidence of a strong Hegelian influence. More specifically, is it an Hegelian argument at all? Or perhaps, more plausibly, what is un-Hegelian about Iqbal's procedure? Quite simply this: that you cannot merely initially state or assert the principle of the unity of thought and being as an empty metaphysical abstraction and then proceed to demonstrate its truth by means of a consideration of the facts of nature as revealed by modern science. The point is well put by Mure: 'Hegel's logic is not formal but Ontological. It is not an abstract thinking in empty disconnected forms which can only get their content through empirical contact with a real world independent of thought' (*The Philosophy of Hegel*, p. 110). Indeed, when we consider the nature and place of this principle within the context of the Hegelian philosophy we shall see how radically Iqbal misunderstands it.

5.7 Hegel on the unity of thought and being

In the exposition of some of the main features of the Hegelian philosophy (see above, p. 14) we have already noted the momentous significance of this idea (the unity of thought and being) in modern philosophy. Its historical roots go back at least to Aristotle. 'For Hegel Aristotle's supreme achievement was his identification of fully substantial being with spirit (*Geist*)' (Mure, *An Introduction to Hegel*, p. 53). Spirit, for Aristotle, was essentially activity — defined as the union of subject and object. Then there were the influences of scholasticism, Descartes, Spinoza and Leibniz. The critical philosophy was an important focus for Hegel but he criticised Kant for subjectivising thought (see Mure, *An Introduction to Hegel*, p. 55). Fichte had come nearer the mark by realising the true sense of the Kantian 'original' unity of apperception, i.e., by virtue of being prior to the thought-being distinction, it is neither subjective nor objective.

A complementary historical approach is the tracing of the antecedents of the Hegelian dialectic. Its 'dialectical precursors' (Mure, *The Philosophy of Hegel*, p. 31) are Socrates, Zeno, Kant and Fichte. Hegel was influenced by all these thinkers but he went beyond them in trying to remedy the one central weakness common to them all, *viz.* dialectic is conceived as the subjective movement of thought which is opposed to the objective world.

5.8

The simplest characterisation of the Hegelian principle of the unity of thought and being is that it is a formula which expresses the nature of reality in a schematic fashion. The Hegelian formulation would run: the principle of the unity of thought and being describes the activity of absolute spirit. Indeed, it is the very nerve and centre of the entire Hegelian endeavour. Such decisive matters as the distinctly Hegelian conceptions of logic, dialectic, and truth can simply not be understood apart from the principle of the unity of thought and being. Mure's insistence (*The Philosophy of Hegel*) that it is at once the presupposition as well as the conclusion of Hegel's philosophy is somewhat misleading. Perhaps the least misleading way of stating the matter is to say that the unity of thought and being is Hegel's profoundest insight into the nature of reality. It is a principle which is seen at work literally everywhere, and at every level of our experience of the world. Thought, which at any stage is only a particular phase in the internal self-movement of the notion or in the perpetual unfolding of self-conscious spirit, is in its very nature neither static nor merely 'abstract' in any simple sense. Thought alienates itself as thought into its other self: being; through a second negation being is reconciled to thought. In this process of self-diremption and self-reconciliation thought *overreaches* and *comprehends* (*übergreift*) being.

The famous dialectic is merely the exemplification of the unity of thought and being throughout all the grades of our experience of the world – from sensuous presentation to imagination, and so on to overt intellectual activity, culminating in the highest forms of the true philosophical thought: logic, nature and spirit. The truth, says Hegel, is the whole ('*das Wahre ist das Ganze*,' Mure, *An Introduction to Hegel*, p. 169). Truth is the correspondence of anything to its Notion; the latter represents the concrete movement of absolute spirit self-dirempting and self-reconciling (thus the integral unity of thought and being is maintained). Truth is constituted by nothing less than the entire assemblage of phases within this spiritual activity of self-knowing.

5.9

Even the categories of Hegelian logic represent nothing other than the self-elaboration of the unity of thought and being at that particular level of the activity of absolute spirit. This is clearly expressed in the following statement in which Hegel is addressing his interlocutors (Mure, *The Philosophy of Hegel*, p. 151):

> But my Logic, as the transition from the *Phenomenology* showed, is the self-consciousness of absolute spirit in its pure and abstract, because immediate, form. In that abstract form it contains – in a sense it *is* – Being as a category. That is because it is self-conscious reason and not understanding which, being independent of its object, has to deny that existence is a predicate. But further, because it is implicitly total and absolute self-consciousness outside which is nothing, it legitimately mediates itself in Nature as in its other self. It legitimately claims the moment of external existence which is its own.

The logical idea represents the first movement in the complete Hegelian system – which he designates as 'the Encyclopaedia of the Philosophical Sciences'.

Nature, in the Hegelian conception, is that phase in the self-development of absolute spirit in which the logical idea as pure, transcendent abstract form, alienates itself to find concrete external embodiment in its other being. Thus the unity of experiencing subject (thought) and object experienced (being) is preserved in the self-externalisation of the idea in nature. This phase constitutes the second movement in the Hegelian system. The logical forms are, however, only imperfectly embodied owing to an element of weakness or impotence in nature. This stage is thus also a dim or approximate prefiguration of the completer self-realisation of spirit in the subsequent stage: the philosophy of spirit. The forms of nature exhibit a hierarchical order but Hegel insists that this does not represent an actual, natural, temporal, process; rather the gradation is of a *logical* character. Here we observe Hegel's impressive fidelity to the factual evidence presented by the natural sciences of his day. Collingwood has pointed out the remarkable affinity between the Hegelian philosophy of nature and that of Whitehead; this view has received more substantial support in the work of Errol E. Harris.

5.10

The Hegelian approach to the proofs of the existence of god is seen *par excellence* in its handling of the ontological proof. It is the finite understanding which is able to dirempt thought from being: the notion of god from that of his existence. Thus there is on the one hand the purely *subjective* idea of god, and on the other, the idea of his *objective* being (existence). But the rational, speculative, infinite philosophical thought culminates in forms which are internally self-complete. Thus man's knowledge of god is at the same time, and more truly, god's knowledge of himself (*via* the circle of the internal self-movement of the Notion). The ordinary proofs of god's existence are merely attempts, inevitably doomed to failure, of the finite understanding to elevate itself to infinity. So far is this the case that the idea of god is itself only a symbolic or pictorial representation of absolute spirit — adequate only to the level of the understanding. Essentially, argues Hegel 'what we have got to do is to show that Being, too, belongs to this Notion'. This leads on naturally, and logically, to a specific exemplification of the unity of thought and being at a higher level. Thus 'in the case of the finite, existence does not correspond to the Notion. On the other hand, in the case of the Infinite, which is determined within itself, the reality must correspond to the Notion; this is the Idea, the unity of subject and object' (*Lectures on the Philosophy of Religion*, vol. 3, p. 362). 'The Notion thus has Being in itself potentially. Its very meaning is that it does away with its one-sidedness. The idea that Being can be separated from the Notion is a mere fancy' (*ibid.*, p. 364). Hegel argues that being is the 'poorest of all abstractions' and therefore there can be no question of the Notion not containing this determination within it (*ibid.*, p.365-6):

> Here it is not a question of any addition of Being to the Notion, or merely of a unity of the Notion and Being — such expressions are awkward and misleading. The unity is rather to be conceived of as an absolute process, as the living movement of God, and this means that

the two sides are distinguished from each other, while the process is thought of as that absolute, continuous act of eternal self-production.

Mure has rightly pointed out (*The Philosophy of Hegel*, p. 150) that Hegel regards his own position as being implicit in Anselm's ontological proof. Thus Hegel writes ('Amplification of the Ontological Proof', pp. 360-7):

The Notion which is only something subjective, and is diverse from Being, is a nullity. In the form of the proof as given by Anselm, the infinity would consist in the very fact that it is not one-sided, something purely subjective to which Being does not attach. The Understanding keeps Being and the Notion strictly apart.

Part II

Iqbal and the Muslim tradition

Praise belongs to God, Who by His magnificence is veiled from the perception of the eyes, and by His glory and might is exalted above the attainment of the thoughts.

Abu Bakr al-Kalabadhi, Proemium to *Doctrine of the Sufis*

Chapter 6

Iqbal and the Quran

6.1

We will now consider some significant examples of Iqbal's attitude to the Quran.

On page 45 of *The Reconstruction* Iqbal reads the Whiteheadian idea of 'Nature's passage in time' into the Quran as 'perhaps the most significant aspect of experience which the Quran especially emphasises.' He refers to three sets of verses quoted by him earlier on, and adds a further five 'in view of the great importance of the subject.' The relevant verses are as follows:[1]

> In the creation of the heavens and the earth, and the alternation of night and day, and the ships that run in the sea with that which profits men, and the water that God sends down from the sky, then gives life therewith to the earth after its death and spreads in it all kinds of animals, and the changing of the winds and the clouds made subservient between heaven and earth, there are surely signs for a people to understand. (2:164)

> In the creation of the heavens and the earth and the alternation of the night and the day, there are surely signs for men of understanding.
> Those who remember God standing and sitting and lying on their sides, and reflect on the creation of the heavens and the earth: Our Lord, Thou hast not created this in vain! Glory be to Thee! Save us from the chastisement of the Fire. (3:189.190)

> Surely in the variation of the night and the day, and that which God has created in the heavens and the earth, there are signs for a people who keep their duty. (10:6)

47

And He it is Who gives life and causes death, and His is the alternation of the night and the day. Do you not then understand? (23:80)

God causes the night and the day to succeed one another. Surely there is a lesson in this for those who have sight. (24:44)

And He it is, Who made the night and the day to follow each other, for him who desires to be mindful or desires to be thankful. (25:62)

Seest thou not that God makes the night to enter into the day, and He makes the day to enter into the night, and He has made the sun and the moon subservient to you — each pursues its course till an appointed time — and that God is Aware of what you do? (31:29)

He has created the heavens and the earth with truth; He makes the night cover the day and makes the day overtake the night, and He has made the sun and the moon subservient; each one moves on to an assigned term. Now surely He is the Mighty, the Forgiver. (39:5)

These verses well represent the Quranic 'natural theology' — the continual reference to order and design in the cosmos: 'signs for men of understanding' (3:189). This has been put succinctly by Abul-Kalam Azad in his masterly commentary on the opening chapter of the Quran: 'What then is the road one should take to seek knowledge of God? The *Quran* says there is but one road to it, and that is to reflect over the phenomenal world of creation.' Further, he relates the order and design in the universe to the divine attributes of providence (*Rububiyat*) and benevolence (*Rahmat*).[2] Another outstanding, but insufficiently appreciated, contemporary commentator, Muhammad Asad, writes with reference to 2:164 (*The Message of the Quran*, p. 34, n. 89):

This passage is one of the many in which the Quran appeals to 'those who use their reason' to observe the daily wonders of nature, including the evidence of man's own ingenuity ('the ships that speed through the sea'), as so many indications of a conscious, creative Power pervading the universe.

There is, however, nothing to suggest that the element of *time* is being particularly emphasised in these verses, and even less is there any specific doctrine or theory of time. Indeed, to read such doctrines and theories into the text is to misunderstand the nature and purpose of the Quranic revelation in a fundamental way. A contemporary Sufi scholar writes: 'for Islam the world is a huge book filled with "signs" (*ayāt*), or symbols — elements of beauty — which speak to our understanding and are addressed to "them that understand".' And again 'the nature which surrounds us − sun, moon, stars, day and night, the seasons, the waters, mountains, forests and flowers − is a kind of primordial Revelation' (Frithjof Schuon, *Understanding Islam*, pp. 40, 58).[3]

6.2

A few pages later (p. 48) Iqbal writes:
The Quran with its characteristic simplicity alludes to the [Bergsonian] serial and non-serial aspects of duration in the following verses:

And put thou thy trust in Him that liveth and dieth not, and celebrate His praise Who in six days created the Heavens and the earth, and what is between them, then mounted His Throne; the God of mercy. 25:58 and 59

All things We have created with a fixed destiny: Our command was but one, swift as the twinkling of an eye. 54:49 and 50

He then comments on these two verses along the lines that the first verse refers metaphorically to the creative process in serial time, whereas the second verse pertains to the 'inner experience of pure duration'. There is no inconsistency, real or apparent, between these two verses and it is neither necessary nor legitimate to foist the Bergsonian theory of time on to them. In any case, god's creative act and his command (*amr*) are referred to separately and it is the latter that 'is but once, as the twinkling of an eye' (Muhammad Ali's translation). This becomes much clearer when we consider an important verse that Iqbal does not quote:

Surely your Lord is God, Who created the heavens and the earth in six periods, and He is established on the Throne of Power. He makes the night cover the day, which it pursues incessantly. And He created the sun and the moon and the stars, made subservient by His command. Surely His is the creation and the command. Blessed is God, the Lord of the worlds! (7:54)

Much light is shed on it by the perceptive comments of the contemporary scholar Fazlur Rahman: 'In the very act of this creation order or "command" is ingrained in things whereby they cohere and fall into a pattern, and rather than "go astray" from the ordained path, evolve into a cosmos' (*Islam*, p. 34).

The most intense impression that the Quran as a whole leaves upon a reader is . . . of a unitary and purposive will creative of order in

49

the universe: the qualities of power or majesty, of watchfulness or justice and of wisdom attributed to God in the Quran with unmistakable emphasis are, in fact, immediate inferences from the creative orderliness of the cosmos. Of all the Quranic terms, perhaps the most basic, comprehensive and revelatory at once of the divine nature of the universe is the term *amr* which we have translated above as order, orderliness or command. To everything that is created is *ipso facto* communicated its *amr* which is its own law of being but which is also a law whereby it is integrated into a system. This *amr*, i.e. order or command of God, is ceaseless.

6.3

Iqbal writes: 'It is time regarded as an organic whole that the Quran describes as "Taqdir" or the destiny — a word which has been so much misunderstood both in and outside the world of Islam (p. 49). The irony here is that it is Iqbal's equation or identification of this Quranic notion with the Bergsonian idea of 'pure time' (on pp. 49, 50) which involves a wholesale misunderstanding of that notion *(Taqdir)*. This is objectionable even from a linguistic point of view, as the word *Taqdir* does not contain any reference to time. A modern commentator, Muhammad Ali, has explained the concept as follows *(The Holy Quran*, pp. 1, 145):

> *Qaddara* (inf. *taqdir*) ordinarily signifies *he made a thing according to a measure*, or *proportioned it*, the significance being that God has allotted to man a certain sphere in which he can make progress. But it sometimes carries the same significance as *aqdara*, viz., *he empowered* him, *enabled* him, *rendered* him *able* (*Lane's Lexicon*), and the meaning in this case would be that Allah has not only created man, but has also given him power and ability, so that he can make progress, if he likes.

Abul-Kalam Azad's commentary is also in line with this: 'The meaning of *Taqdir* is "to assign" a particular role to everything, whether quantitatively or qualitatively' *(The Tarjuman al-Quran*, p. 27).

6.4

Iqbal's arbitrary way of interpreting the Quranic text recurs again when he formulates (p. 56) his notion of 'the ultimate Self'. We shall have occasion to comment on the weakness of his case here (see chapter 8). The ultimate self (or the absolute ego) includes nature as an organic part of its own self. But nature is also a human interpretation 'put on the creative activity of the Absolute Ego'. No adequate conception can be formed of such a self. Iqbal tries to find Quranic support for such an incoherent position.

(1) 'Nothing is like Him; and He is the Hearing, the Seeing' (42:11). This verse has far more radical implications than suggested by Iqbal's very weak rendering, i.e., that only an inadequate conception can be formed of god. The commentator Muhammad Ali emphasises that it conveys the sense of God's supreme transcendence. 'The words translated *like him* literally mean *like a likeness of Him*', so much so that god is 'even above *the limitation of metaphor*' (*The Holy Quran*, p. 918).

(2) Nature is an organic part of the divine self. 'In the picturesque phrase of the Quran it is the habit of Allah.' There is nothing picturesque about this phrase, which has been misquoted, mistranslated and misunderstood by Iqbal. The word refers, in fact, to *human communities* and not to nature in Iqbal's sense. This meaning is quite plain. Fazlur Rahman writes: 'The Quran also speaks of the Sunna of God, i.e. the behaviour of God with reference to the pattern or fate of societies — a behaviour which is unalterable' (*Islam*, p. 44). Muhammad Ali also translates the term (*Sunnah*) in the same spirit. His rendering is, to take two examples:

That was the way of Allah concerning those who have gone before; and thou wilt find no change in the way of Allah. (33:62)

But thou wilt find no alteration in the course of Allah; and thou wilt find no change in the course of Allah. (35:43)

He explains : '*Sunan* is plural of *sunnah*, meaning *a way* or *rule* or *manner of acting* or *conduct* or *life* or *the like* (Lane's Lexicon). Hence the significance here is *ways* or *examples* of *Allah's dealing with the righteous and the wicked*' (*The Holy Quran*, p. 167).

(3) The only limit to the ever-growing organism of nature is internal, 'the immanent Self which animates and sustains the whole. As the Quran says: "And verily unto thy Lord is the limit" (53:42)'. Wrong again — 'the limit' is a mistranslation; in any case, the reference is not to the natural world but to the moral and spiritual striving of man. Thus, in the full context, the verses read (53:38-42, Muhammad Ali, *The Holy Quran*, p. 1,005)

That no bearer of a burden bears another's burden:
And that man can have nothing but what he strives for:

And that his striving will soon be seen.
Then he will be rewarded for it with the fullest reward:
And that to thy Lord is the goal.

A great contemporary Sufi, Shaikh Ahmad Al-Alawi (died 1934), writes in the same vein (M. Lings, *A Sufi Saint of the Twentieth Century*, p. 147):

> Other than God will not vanish at a mere 'no' upon the tongue, nor yet through the eye of faith and certainty but only when thou comest unto the station of direct perception and face-to-face vision; and verily *thy Lord is the Uttermost End* (53:42), unto which all cometh.

6.5

To take one final, and important, example of Iqbal's reference to the Quran: he quotes the opening lines of the famous 'light' verse. The entire verse reads:

> God is the light of the heavens and the earth. A likeness of His light is as a pillar on which is a lamp — the lamp is in a glass, the glass is as it were a brightly shining star — lit from a blessed olive-tree, neither eastern nor western, the oil whereof gives light, though fire touch it not — light upon light. God guides to His light whom He pleases. And God sets forth parables for men, and God is knower of all things. (24:35)

Iqbal comments on this verse along the lines that it involves an 'identification of God with light' (p. 63). His comments are overly concrete and literal: 'the development of the metaphor is meant rather to exclude the suggestion of a formless cosmic element by centralizing the light in a flame which is further individualised by its encasement in a glass likened unto a well-defined star.' There is no 'identification of God with light': the Quran refers plainly to 'His light'; and, indeed, further: '*A likeness of* His light'.

Iqbal goes on to assert that the light metaphor must now be re-interpreted according to the findings of modern physics: 'The teaching of modern physics is that the velocity of light cannot be exceeded ... light is the nearest approach to the Absolute.' Therefore the light metaphor 'must be taken to suggest the Absoluteness of God'. The velocity of light is a limit only in the special theory of relativity, as distinct from the general theory of relativity. Even so, this limit is a matter of convention – or, put more technically, it is a topological postulate of the special theory of relativity (see Adolf Grünbaum, 'Philosophical significance of relativity theory', *Encyclopaedia of Philosophy*, vol. 7). Therefore, the rest of Iqbal's thesis does not, and cannot, follow from this fact. In any case, this kind of approach to understanding the symbology of the Quran is clearly self-defeating, for any absolute limits in science, and the notion of god as 'the Absolute' (whether Hegelian or not) or 'the Absoluteness of God', are obviously two very different things. The similarity is merely verbal, whereas the dissimilarity is profound: one word pertains to the finite human sphere, whereas the other refers to that of 'the Infinite'.

Chapter 7

Muslim theism: the classical formulation of the orthodox doctrine by al-Ghazali and Abul-Kalam Azad

7.1 Preliminary: the nature and the sources of our knowledge of God

The issues of the nature and the sources of our knowledge of God are interrelated. The question of the sources is primary, and crucial. The matter of the nature of the knowledge derived from those sources raises issues that are both logical as well as epistemological, and it will be proper to deal with these under the general heading of 'The Nature of the Problem of God' (see part III).

Mankind has derived its knowledge of god from the three great sources of reason, revelation and religious experience. These three components are mutually complementary and totally exhaustive. They are mutually interdependent but each component may also function, to different degrees, in a relatively autonomous manner. Reason, both in the narrow sense of the intellective, ratiocinative, discursive faculty, as well as the wider sense to include such processes as understanding and interpretation, is basic.[1] Without reason, no sense could possibly be made of revelation or religious experience. The diverse modes of God's self-disclosure to man constitute revelation. Among recent writers Ninian Smart has particularly emphasised that revelation is not merely 'a string of propositions infallibly uttered by God' (*Philosophers and Religious Truth*, p. 21). Rather, it must be seen as a personal encounter between God and man. But there is no real difficulty here — Smart's caveat is redundant, and is in fact arrived at by a violation of one of his own most cherished premises, *viz.* the Wittgensteinian idea (Wittgenstein II) that language operates within a living context (*Lebensform*: a form of life). Thus, to a Muslim the self-revelatory propositions of God in the Quran live in the multiple context of the Quranic theology and his own attitude to belief and practice. Religious experience ranges along an extensive continuum – from the sense of God's presence in the ordinary believer's act of worship at one end to Otto's *sensus numinis* and mystical experience at the other extreme. This raises the whole complex and difficult problem of experience and the interpretation of experience: we will deal with it in chapter 10.

These three components interact in different ways in particular thinkers. Take a few examples. Revelation is the supreme and final authority for al-Ghazali. His exercise of reason and his mystical experience are the means to understand and interpret the deliverances of revelation. For Plotinus, reason is the prime source of truth and this is confirmed in mystical experience. In the case of Sankara and Eckhart mystical experience is the centrally important thing, and this experience is subjected to elaborate interpretation in terms of the religious doctrines obtaining in their respective cultures. Reason reigns supreme in Bradley's thought, and he opposes the results of intellectual inquiry to religious doctrine (Christian theism).

Iqbal accepts the relative autonomy of reason while taking revelation as the rock upon which the structure of religion is built. He writes in chapter 1 of *The Reconstruction* 'Knowledge and religious experience', p. 2:

> But to rationalise faith is not to admit the superiority of philosophy over religion. Philosophy, no doubt, has jurisdiction to judge religion, but what is to be judged is of such a nature that it will not submit to the jurisdiction of philosophy except on its own terms. . . . Thus, in the evaluation of religion, philosophy must recognise the central position of religion and has no other alternative but to admit it as something focal in the process of reflective synthesis.

He makes some interesting observations on the nature of mystical experience and also accepts its cognitive validity.

7.2 al-Ghazali

The orthodox Muslim tradition teaches a doctrine of God's supreme transcendence while emphasising, at the same time, his closeness to man: 'we are nearer to Him than His life-vein' (50:16). I call on two major representatives to expound their own formulation of this doctrine. First, al-Ghazali (died 1111 – thus a contemporary of Anselm) who, by the almost universal consensus of Muslim scholars, is one of the greatest minds — both in a spiritual and an intellectual sense — produced by Islam. He combined the roles of lawyer, philosopher, theologian and mystic, and is quite appropriately known as the *Hujjat al-Islam* (the Proof of Islam).[2]

Al-Ghazali states the doctrine as follows:[3]

> Praise be to God, the creator . . . He is one in essence, unequalled, unique, sole, incomparable, alone without opponent or rival. He exists from the beginning, without predecessor, from all eternity, beginningless; he endures, none follows him, he is everlasting without end. . . He is no substance and there are no substances in him; he is not an accident and there are no accidents in him. . . He is high above heaven and earth, and yet is 'closer to a man than his own arteries' . . . for his presence is not like that of a body . . . he is not in things nor are things in him. . . In his essence no other thing can exist, nor can his essence be in anything outside him. He is exalted above change and alteration; for him there are no happenings, no misfortune can befall him, but rather he possesses everlastingly the properties of his majesty, beyond the reach of decay, and for the attributes of his perfection he needs no growth or process of perfecting.

I shall comment on al-Ghazali's position in chapter 12, on 'The nature of our knowledge of god'.

7.3 Abul-Kalam Azad

The other representative is a contemporary (died 1959), Abul-Kalam Azad, probably the most outstanding scholar produced by Indian (in the sense of the whole subcontinent) Islam in this century. His views have been fully and clearly stated in the course of his commentary on the opening chapter of the Quran.[4]

After an extensive historical and comparative survey of the origins and development of the idea of god Azad states of the Quranic teaching that 'it embodies a comprehensive concept of the unity of God. . . . From the standpoint of anthropomorphism versus transcendentalism, the Quranic concept of the transcendental assumes a state of perfection, such as had not been reached before' (p. 127).

Prior to the Quran the human intellect could not get beyond the replacement of image-worship by the worship of 'an unseen God'. The

ascription of 'divine attributes' to the deity could not avoi
morphism. Thus (ibid.):

> we find in the *Old Testament* very fine attributes applied to
> along with qualities and passions intensely human. *Even Chri*   ...
> he desired to speak of the universal mercy of God, was obliged to
> employ the similitude of relationship subsisting between father and
> son.

A radically new departure is made by the Quran.

> All the veils of anthropomorphic similitudes are lifted and transcen-
> dentalism glows in perfection:
> Nought is there like Him (42:11).
> No vision taketh Him in
> But He taketh in all vision (6:103).
> Say: He is God, the one only:
> God, on whom all depend!
> He begetteth not, nor is He begotten;
> And there is none like Him (112:1-4).

The affirmation of divine attributes can lead to anthropomorphism
whereas the process of negation (such as the Upanishadic *Neti Neti*) can
lead to 'total nullification'. 'The aim of the *Quran* is to present a perfect
transcendental vision of God', and hence it 'has chosen the middle path'.

The Quran affirms a wide variety of individual attributes through the
use of figurative expressions and metaphors, while countering every
form of anthropomorphic representation. Thus, for example:

> Surely My Lord is watchful. (89:14)

> And when My servant asks thee concerning me, then will I be nigh
> unto him. I will answer the cry of him that crieth, when he crieth
> unto me. (2:186)

> Nay, both His hands are spread out. (5:64)

> His knowledge extends over the heavens and the earth. (2:255)

At the same time the Quran is explicit about the uniquely incomparable nature of god:

> Nought is there like Him. (42:11)

> No vision taketh Him in. (6:103)

> So coin not similitudes for Him. (16:74)

Azad comments (pp. 130-1):

His "living" is not like our living, His "Providence" is not like our providence, His "seeing" or "hearing" or "knowing" is not like ours. The metaphor of hand is used only to denote His power and forgiveness, and that of *Arsh* to denote his majesty and his control. But the sense is not the same as may be formed of them in our mind in respect of their relation to human activity.

The problem of divine attributes was the subject of protracted and intricate disquisitions among Muslim theologians and philosophers. Azad writes (pp. 131-2):

When a solution was furnished, it was furnished in the manner of the *Quran*. Imam Fakhruddin Razi of the School of Ashari, who took a leading part in the controversy, had ultimately to admit in his last work: 'I employed all the methods which philosophy and dialectic had provided, but in the end I realised that these methods neither could bring solace to the weary heart nor quench the thirst of the thirsty. The best method and the nearest to reality was the method provided by the *Quran*.'

Hence many early authorities 'adopted the attitude of *Tafwid* or of submission, whereby they could affirm and believe in what was stated of God in the *Quran* but suspend judgement concerning it and offer no interpretations thereof' (p. 132).

The Quran divides its verses into two categories: *Muhkamat* and *Mutashabihat*. The former are clear and unequivocal whereas the latter are figurative. According to Azad (p. 133):

The attributes are to be treated as *Mutashabihat* (figurative). So, the *Quran* considers intellectual effort to comprehend them as fruitless. Indeed, they will open the door for doubts and misrepresentations. *Tafwid* is the only attitude appropriate to the situation, the attitude of affirmation and belief in them and suspension of judgement. All the philosophic disquisitions, which our dialecticians have indulged in, are not in conformity with the teaching of the *Quran*.

Chapter 8

Muslim panentheism: the modernist 'reconstruction' of the Quranic doctrine by Muhammad Iqbal

8.1

Essentially and fundamentally Iqbal has developed a finite[1] conception of deity. Most specifically, and crucially, he has argued for the inclusion of the created order (nature) within the being of the creator (god). And we are not left in any doubt as to the manner in which we are to conceptualise this process of inclusion – nature is an organic part of 'the Ultimate Self'. Iqbal designates this position as 'pantheistic'. If we understand by this term that God and the world form a unity, and that this united whole is divine, then it is a reasonably accurate characterisation of his view.[2] Strictly speaking it is a panentheistic position.[3] But then Iqbal also goes on to argue that his notion of nature as 'a rationally directed creative life' is to be interpreted as *an ego*: this incoherent formulation at least sounds more like straightforward pantheism. The difficulty is compounded further by Iqbal's equation, or identification, of his 'Absolute Ego'[4] with the Quranic conception of God. And yet he admits that, 'of such a Self it is impossible for us to form an adequate conception. As the *Quran* says, "Nought is like Him; yet He hears and sees".' Such is the logical conclusion of the tension, and, in fact, the incoherence and the inconsistency, inherent in his case. If, indeed, Iqbal had grasped the true significance of the Quranic doctrine he himself invokes – the insistence on the incomparable uniqueness of god ('Nothing is like Him; and He is the Hearing, the Seeing' (42:11)) – he would have found it utterly impossible even to begin to develop his own theory.

In his chapter III ('The conception of god and the meaning of prayer') Iqbal emphasises the egohood of the 'Ultimate Ego' – so much so that he is expressly against pantheistic modes of thought. Thus he argues that the famous 'light' verse in the Quran (24:35) must be taken as a

59

metaphor 'To suggest the Absoluteness of God and not His Omnipresence which easily lends itself to a pantheistic interpretation' (p. 64). At the same time he does not want to compromise his view of 'the ultimate ground of all experience, a rationally directed creative will' (p. 62). So the tension and incoherence as between the various distinct positions (pantheism): Iqbal's 'Ultimate Ego': the Quranic God) remain. Be that as it may, Iqbal's discussion of god's egohood and infinitude and the divine attributes (creativeness, eternity, knowledge and omnipotence) all reinforce his fundamentally finite notion of deity. Especially noteworthy here are the following statements:

(a) Space and time are interpretations put by finite human thought on the ultimate ego's creative activity. 'Beyond Him and apart from His creative activity there is neither time nor space to close Him off in reference to other egos' (p. 64).

(b) 'The question of creation once arose among the disciples of the well-known saint Ba Yazid of Bistam. One of the disciples very pointedly put the common sense view saying: 'There is a moment of time when God existed and nothing else existed beside Him.' The saint's reply was equally pointed. 'It is just the same now', said he, 'as it was then.' The world of matter, therefore, is not a stuff co-eternal with God, operated upon by Him from a distance as it were. It is, in its real nature, one continuous act which thought breaks up into a plurality of mutually exclusive things' (pp. 65, 66). [Abu Yazid al-Bistami's (died 874) reply amounts to a succinct formulation of the central Sufi doctrine of *Wahdat al-Wujud*, or Oneness of Being.] [5]

(c) The universe does not confront God as an 'other' existing *per se* ... from the standpoint of the all-inclusive Ego there is no 'other'. In Him thought and deed, the act of knowing and the act of creating, are identical (p. 77).

8.2

Basically Iqbal's procedure involves two moves. First, he draws some quite unreasonably extravagant, and indeed, in some very important respects, illegitimate, metaphysical conclusions from his philosophical inquiry into modern science and philosophy. I have tried to demonstrate this in the first part of this work. The second move is his repeated and persistent attempt to read the results of his inquiry into the Quran. This second move was considered in chapter 6.

We have already observed (part I) the influence of such leading western philosophers as Hegel, Whitehead and Bergson on Iqbal. The Hegelian influence was shown to be specifically in the areas of epistemology and metaphysics. It may be worth while to inquire into the precise nature and extent of the Hegelian influence in the development of Iqbal's conception of god.[6]

As already indicated (part I, chapters 4 and 5) the Bergsonian influence has been decisive in the formulation of Iqbal's doctrine of God. I have also tried to show that Iqbal's extension of Bergsonian ideas is unwarranted by the French philosopher's own statement of his views. In general, it was observed that his discussions of modern science and philosophy were inadequate – lacking in both depth and rigour – as well as being unoriginal. In the present context, I wish to point out one specific weakness in Iqbal's case: one, indeed, which concerns the very core of his attempt to derive the concept of god from Bergsonian premises. It is far from clear how Bergsonian 'appreciative intuition' yields the knowledge of the nature of God. Is god Iqbal's 'ultimate reality' as thus intuited? Or is the notion of God arrived at by some process of analogical reasoning? *Both* positions seem to be contained in Iqbal's arguments. In either case the crucial difficulty is this: How is the *transition* (or transcension) from man to God achieved? There is no answer to this question. Iqbal's case must surely founder on this rock.

8.3

Hartshorne and Reese, in their *Philosophers Speak of God*, include Iqbal in their chapter on 'Modern panentheism'[7] – alongside such thinkers as Schelling, Whitehead, Berdyaev and Radhakrishnan. In his introductory note Hartshorne remarks that despite the strong influence of western thinkers on Iqbal 'the eloquence and sincerity of the numerous references to Moslem sources are no less striking'. Further, since, in the view of the authors, no particular religion is adequately represented by classical theism, 'There is for us no absurdity or paradox in a panentheistic version of Islam' (p. 294). Unfortunately, eloquence and sincerity have never been, and indeed could never be, a guarantee of the soundness or validity of the ideas they convey. Iqbal's own eloquence and sincerity in quoting Muslim sources, and especially the Quran, are not in question, but the issue of their cogency is quite a different matter. My principal charge here against Iqbal is that he has taken great liberties in quoting the Quran – it is done in a wholly gratuitous manner and without any regard for the Muslim tradition of *Tafsir* (exegesis) and *Kalam* (theology). The most conspicuous example of this procedure is the attempt to interpret Quranic references to the alternation of day and night in terms of the Bergsonian doctrine of pure duration.[8]

8.4

Iqbal's doctrine of god is panentheistic — although, as we have already noticed, he calls it pantheistic. On the other hand, he is distinctly uncomfortable that his intellectual inquiries should end in such a view. Hence the laboured attempt to argue that such a divine being (nature as 'a rationally directed creative life', p. 60) must be conceived of as an ego. The overall result is that Iqbal is quite unable to resolve the tension and incoherence in his case. The crucial point from the viewpoint of Muslim orthodoxy is simply the fact that Iqbal is defending a *finite* conception of God — and such a god cannot be reconciled with the plain doctrine of the Quran.

It is remarkable that Iqbal's conception of God is very close to that which has been considered the norm in Sufi orthodoxy. Both are in effect, even if not by deliberate design, finite conceptions: one is panentheistic and the other is pantheistic,[9] but here again the relationship is more intimate, as seen earlier on, than is commonly supposed. It is clearly a matter of great interest that Iqbal and the Sufis should — though having distinct origins and traversing different routes — eventually converge on what is, in effect, virtually a common destination. Quite apart from its intrinsic interest and importance — which is very considerable — this fact alone provides sufficient warrant for examining the Sufi doctrine of God.

A word about Iqbal's own attitude to Sufism would be in order here. On the evidence of *The Reconstruction* Iqbal's attitude to Sufism was complex. Thus, on the one hand he defends the genuine cognitive validity of mystical experience (chapter 1, 'Knowledge and religious experience'), while on the other hand, he expresses views that are sometimes critical and sometimes ambivalent. Thus, for instance (p. 90):

> Mysticism has, no doubt, revealed fresh regions of the self by
> making a special study of this experience [the experience of prayer].
> Its literature is illuminating; yet its set phraseology, shaped by the
> thought-forms of a worn-out metaphysics, has rather a deadening
> effect on the modern mind.

Later on (chapter 6, 'The principle of movement in the structure of Islam') he attributes the stagnant state of Muslim Law to three principal causes — the second one being the development within Sufism 'under influences of a non-Islamic character, [of] a purely speculative side', as distinct from 'its purely religious side' of which he evidently approves (p. 150).

There is no explicit reference to the Sufi doctrine of *Wahdat al-Wujud* (Oneness of Being), although he does mention 'Pantheistic Sufism' at least once (p. 180), and criticises it. It is of interest to note that at least two of Iqbal's Sufi quotations amount to a statement of *Wahdat al-Wujud*, although he himself seems unaware of this. (1) Abu Yazid al-Bistami (p. 65) noted above in section 8.1 (b). (2) Ibn al-Arabi: 'God is a percept; the world is a concept' (p. 183). Also relevant here is the suggestion that Iqbal followed Ahmad Sirhindi in rejecting the doctrine of *Wahdat al-Wujud*.[10]

Chapter 9

Muslim pantheism: the contemporary exposition of the Sufi doctrine by Isa Nuruddin (Schuon) and Abubakr Sirajuddin (Lings)[1]

9.1 Isa Nuruddin

The doctrine of *Wahdat al-Wujud*, or Oneness of Being, [2] was first formulated by the celebrated Spanish Sufi, Ibn al-Arabi (died 1240).[3] It has been upheld by Sufis over the centuries. One notable exception was the great Indian Sufi Ahmad Sirhindi (died 1625). We shall have occasion to refer to his critique of this doctrine (part III).

The distinguished Swiss Sufi Monsieur Frithjof Schuon (Isa Nuruddin) is an important contemporary representative of Ibn al-Arabi's doctrine. He has been followed, rather uncritically, by a number of well-known scholars — among them Titus Burckhardt, Martin Lings and Seyyed Hossein Nasr. It would be convenient first to consider Schuon's brief statement of the doctrine and then to assess its detailed elaboration by Martin Lings.

In his *Understanding Islam* Schuon writes (pp. 16-17):[4]

The doctrine of Islam hangs on two statements: first — 'There is no divinity (or reality, or absolute) outside the only Divinity (or Reality, or Absolute). (*La ilaha illa 'Llah*), and 'Muhammad (the "Glorified", the Perfect) is the Envoy (the mouthpiece, the intermediary, the manifestation, the symbol) of the Divinity' (*Muhammadun Rasulu 'Llah*); these are the first and the second 'Testimonies' (*Shahadat*) of the faith.

Here we have two assertions which implicate 'two levels of reality: the Absolute and the relative, Cause and effect, God and the world'. Islam is based on these 'two axiomatic certainties': one concerns 'the Principle', ('which is both Being and Beyond-Being'), and the other concerns the manifestation, ('both formal and supraformal'). This is a matter of 'God' – or 'the Godhead' in the Eckhartian sense – on the one hand and of 'Earth' and 'Heaven' on the other. 'The first of these certainties is that "God alone is" and the second that "all things are attached to God".'

The word 'Divinity' (*ilah*) in the first testimony designates the world: It is unreal because God alone is real. The Prophet's name (*Muhammad*) in the second testimony also designates the world: 'it is real because nothing can be outside God; in certain respects all is He.' Realising the first testimony involves the full awareness of the fact that 'the Principle alone is real and that the world, though on its own level it "exists", "is not".' Similarly, the second testimony means that the world is 'not other' than God, 'since to the degree that it has reality it can only be that which alone "is", or in other words it can only be divine; realizing this *Shahadah* thus means seeing God everywhere and everything in Him' (p. 17).

The above statement contains the essentials of Schuon's position.[5] He is expounding the fundamental credo of Islam – the *Kalimah Shahadah* (the Word of Confession or Testimony): in effect it amounts to an exposition of the Sufi doctrine of God (*Wahdat al-Wujud*). If we distil out the essence of this doctrine from Schuon's statement, we find that it consists of the dual assertion that:

(1) The only reality is God, and there can be nothing outside God ('all is He').

(2) The world therefore 'can only be divine'.

Further analysis of this position yields:

(1) The God-world dualism has been abolished. Therefore it is a *monistic* position.

(2) The resulting complex (God-world) unity, however, is divine. Therefore it is a *pantheistic* position.[6]

Hence, we can characterise Schuon's doctrine quite precisely as *pantheistic monism*.

However, in *The Transcendent Unity of Religions* (pp. 53-6) Schuon argues that his position is *not* a pantheistic one. He commences by expressing the view that the most important idea in his *esoteric* perspective which is not available in the *exoteric* one is that of 'the gradation of universal Reality: Reality affirms itself by degrees, and without ceasing to be "one", the inferior degrees of this "affirmation" being absorbed, by metaphysical integration or synthesis, into the superior degree.'[7]

Thus, Schuon writes of 'the doctrine of the cosmic illusion': the world does not exist since God is the sole Reality. But there is something *higher* than 'the "Personal God"' — 'the "Impersonal" or "Supra-Personal Divinity", "Non-Being" of which the "Personal God" or Being is simply the first determination'. So we have here 'the transcendence of the supreme Divine Impersonality of which God is the personal Affirmation'. Exotericism cannot understand these matters since 'such truths are of too high an order, and therefore too subtle and too complex from the point of view of simple rational understanding'. Similarly with the Eckhartian idea of 'the immanence in all beings of the Intellect, which Meister Eckhart defined as "uncreated and uncreatable"', which seems to be related to 'the idea of metaphysical realisation' whereby man becomes aware of 'his essential identity with the Divine Principle which alone is real. Exotericism on the other hand, is obliged to maintain the distinction between Lord and servant, leaving aside the fact that the profanely-minded affect to see in the metaphysical idea of essential identity nothing but 'pantheism', which incidentally relieves them of any effort at comprehension.' Pantheism is defined by Schuon as consisting 'in the admission of a continuity between the Infinite and the finite'. This is quite acceptable but then he goes on to assert, quite arbitrarily, that such a continuity is only conceivable on the basis of a 'substantial' identity between God ('the ontological Principle — which is in question in all forms of Theism') and the world. This involves either a false (substantial) idea of Being, or a confusion of substantial with essential identity. 'Pantheism is this and nothing else.' So Schuon is here making, implicitly, some kind of fundamental distinction between the 'substantial' and the 'essential' aspects of 'existence'. *However, he does not define these terms.* He goes on to assert that the position of those who affirm 'the "existence" of God . . . against an imaginary pantheism prove [s] that their conception is not even truly theistic, since it does not attain to Being'. Finally, it is important to note that Schuon uses the expression 'the ontological Principle' in this discussion in the sense (quite clear in the context) of Being — which is 'the purely essential aspect' of existence.

Now this is a rather naïve and intellectually immature exercise on Monsieur Schuon's part. The terms that he uses so arbitrarily, and without troubling to specify their meaning, have in fact acquired considerable weight within the western philosophical and theological tradition. (For instance. Anselm identifies Being with essence, and Aqinas Being with *esse* or existence, and both identify God with Being. See, for instance, E. L. Mascall, *He Who Is*, p. xi.) However, it is clear, as noted above, that Schuon uses the terms *'ontology'* ('the ontological Principle') and Being in a correlative manner and this accords with the traditional usage.

So the upshot of Schuon's argument is that the *'essential'* identity of God and the world *involves an ontological God-world continuity*, since essence pertains to Being. And this *is* a pantheistic position, even on his own definition. (Strictly speaking Schuon's definition is not sufficiently specific, and his attempt to make it more specific only involves, as already observed, an arbitrary qualification.) We are therefore bound to reject Monsieur Schuon's quibble over the distinction between 'essential' and 'substantial' identity as an irrelevant verbal move, and a rather elementary one at that.

Two additional considerations reinforce the view that Schuon's theory is essentially and fundamentally pantheistic. First, the reference to Eckhart is suspect. He is generally regarded as being the most philosophical and the most controversial of Christian mystics, and his doctrine of God is very similar to, and probably identical with, the pantheistic teaching of Sankara (see, for instance, W. T. Stace, *Mysticism and Philosophy*, p. 224; Ninian Smart, *Philosophers and Religious Truth*, p. 130). Second, and more overtly, there is a vitally important comment made by Schuon on Ibn al-Arabi in his *Understanding Islam*, in the section we have examined above (its relegation to a footnote is undeserved). Quite paradoxically, he asserts that Ibn al-Arabi's doctrine 'was essentially Mohammadan and was in particular even a sort of commentary on *Muhammadun Rasulu 'Llah* in the meaning of the Vedantic sayings: "all things are Atma" and "That art thou"' (p. 18). There could not be a plainer, or indeed bolder, equation of a central Muslim belief with Hindu pantheism.[8]

9.2 Abubakr Sirajuddin

We will now examine Martin Lings's (Abubakr Sirajuddin) formulation and defence of the doctrine in his *A Sufi Saint of the Twentieth Century* (ch. V, 'The oneness of being'),[9] with particular reference to the Quran and the *Hadith* (the Prophet's Traditions or sayings), and an important work by al-Ghazali, *Mishkat al-Anwar* (*The Niche for Lights*).

9.2 (1)

Lings's preliminary remarks betray his excessive zeal to establish the importance and the universality of the Sufi doctrine of the Oneness of Being (*Wahdat al-Wujud*). Thus the chapter opens with a quotation from the late Professor R. A. Nicholson of Cambridge on the lines that, 'Mysticism in all ages and countries is fundamentally the same.' Now as regards mysticism being the same phenomenon everywhere this is at least a great oversimplification. Some important writers do take this view, e.g., W. T. Stace and Ninian Smart, but the opposition is by no means negligible, e.g., Rudolf Otto and R. C. Zaehner, E. G. Parrinder has, in a notably lucid contribution 'Definitions of Mysticism' to the continuing debate, emphasised the complexity of the issues involved here. But as far as Lings's own assertion is concerned it is quite simply false. No such doctrine occurs, for instance, in early Buddhism, or in contemporary Theravada Buddhism. Even in Hinduism it appears in a clear and full-blown form only in the teaching of Sankara.[10]

The doctrine is stated as follows (p. 122):

> Oneness of Being is the doctrine that behind the illusory veil of created plurality there lies the one Divine Truth – not that God is made up of parts, but that underlying each apparently separate feature of the created universe there is the One Infinite Plenitude of God in His Indivisible Totality.

The ambiguity in such terms as 'behind' and 'underlying' is removed in the subsequent elaboration. Lings comments: 'If there were anything which in the Reality of the Eternal Present, could show itself to be other than God, then God would not be Infinite, for Infinity would consist of God *and* that particular thing' (p. 123). Now this is an incoherent, and indeed, arguably even a self-contradictory, statement. If 'the Infinite' includes the reality of the world in His Being then quite clearly we are dealing with a *finite* God. On the other hand it is perfectly coherent, and logically sound, to assert that God, as Infinite Being or Creator, stands *over against* the finite created order that is the world. And further – 'this doctrine is only concerned with Absolute Reality. It has nothing to do with "reality" in the current sense, that is, with lesser, relative truths which the Sufis call "metaphorical".' '"Reality" in the current sense' so far from being metaphorical is the only concrete, proper and literal way of understanding the word. To call it a metaphor is nothing less than perverse. So much so that the notion of 'Absolute Reality' can acquire some kind of oblique reference, say to God, only by way of metaphor – and this is possible only because the word *reality* is already firmly anchored to its direct and straightforward meaning in our *ordinary* experience.

9.2 (2)

We now move on to consider Lings's all-important endeavour to adduce Quranic support for his doctrine. This is in two parts, and the second part also refers to the Prophet's Traditions (*Hadith*). The first part runs as follows (pp. 121-2):

As it is to be expected in view of its centrality, some of the most perfect, though elliptical, formulations of this doctrine are to be found in the *Quran*, which affirms expressly: *Wheresoe'er ye turn, there is the Face of God* (2:115). *Everything perisheth but His Face* (28:88). *All that is therein suffereth extinction, and there remaineth the Face of thy Lord in Its Majesty and Bounty* (55:26-27). Creation, which is subject to time and space and non-terrestrial modes of duration and extent which the human imagination cannot grasp, is 'then' (with reference to both past and future) and 'there', but it is never truly 'now' and 'here'. The True Present is the prerogative of God Alone, for It is no less than the Eternity and Infinity which transcends, penetrates and embraces all durations and extents, being not only 'before' all beginnings but also 'after' all ends. In It, that is, in the Eternal Now and Infinite Here, all that is perishable has 'already' perished, all that is liable to extinction has 'already' been extinguished leaving only God, and it is to this Divine Residue, the Sole Lord of the Present that the word *remaineth* refers in the last quoted Quranic verse.

Before scrutinising these important Quranic verses some general comments would be in order. They clearly refer to such ideas as God's Supreme Transcendence, Eternity, Infinity and Omnipresence – so that we, and the whole order of creation, are as nothing before the Majesty and Glory of God. Lings's own comment, which seems to have a peculiarly attractive quality could, and quite properly should, be taken as a *poetic* evocation of the self-same divine attributes. No particular difficulty is presented if the matter is seen in this way – and, indeed, as already indicated, I would urge that this *is* the correct sense and spirit in which to approach the Quranic verses in question. But, equally clearly, Lings himself dissents from this way of understanding them, for in his view they constitute 'some of the most perfect, though elliptical, formulations of this doctrine'. But do they? The answer is by no means as easily in the affirmative as Lings's attitude would suggest. If, indeed, such extravagant, and even fantastic, interpretations are to be put on these verses they can be sustained only by violating the most cardinal doctrines of the Quranic theology. What could usefully be termed the *fundamental categorial scheme* of the Quran is plain enough. This categorial scheme is embedded in the cultural matrix of the whole Semitic tradition, so much so that in the Muslim perspective, Islam is an organic development of the Judaeo-Christian base — being nothing less than a logical extension and spiritual synthesis of its deepest insights. It is the claim of the Quran, and therefore an article of faith with Muslims, that its teaching represents the perfect culmination, and thus the spiritual consummation, of the Judaeo-Christian message.[11] It is essential to keep this background in mind, for it then becomes evident that any violation of the Quranic categorial scheme implies, *ipso facto*, a violation of all those fundamental elements in the categorial scheme of its sister religions, Judaism and Christianity, which are shared by it; or, put another way, which are held in common as part and parcel of the whole Semitic tradition in mankind's religious culture.

The fundamental categorial scheme of the Quran is contained in the opening chapter.[12] The elements of the scheme distil out easily. Thus we find a set of basic logical categories, or ultimate particulars, set within a network of interrelated propositions. This logical categorisation is the fourfold one of *God*, *World* (or cosmos), *Man* (and, by extension, the history of nations and communities), and the *Path* (the right path: that of moral and spiritual development). The logical distinctions here involved are fundamental, absolute and final. It follows logically that the doctrine of the Oneness of Being would impugn this major premise.

One other consideration is relevant here. We have already noted (section 7.3) the rule of interpretation provided by the Quran on the basis that some of its verses are decisive (*Muhkam*) whereas others are allegorical (*Mutashabih*) (Quran 3:6). It was also observed that as astute a modern scholar as Abul-Kalam Azad was of the view that all the Quranic specifications of the Divine Nature and Attributes should be seen as belonging to the category of allegorical allusion (*Mutashabihat*). Those verses which provide the fundamental categorial scheme, or in various ways elaborate on it, must, and clearly do, belong to the former (decisive) group. On the other hand, the verses on which Lings bases his theory, and many other kindred verses, clearly fall into the latter (allegorical) group.

The corpus of the Prophet's Traditions (*Hadith*) is an extension of the Quran by way of providing more detailed elucidation on points of both doctrine and practice. Therefore it is necessarily subject to, and subsumed under, the general framework I have just outlined.

These considerations provide the essential guidelines in the interpretation and understanding of the relevant Quranic verses. They also constitute, I submit, a powerful *a priori* argument against Lings's case. It must also follow, as a corollary, that anything like the doctrine Lings is propounding can only be arrived at by the assumption of a liberty which is as wholly arbitrary as it is entirely gratuitous. We return now to the text of the Quran.

Lings's translation is questionable, and, more seriously, he has in all three cases removed the verses from their context. In fact the verse is quoted intact only in the third quotation. The first quotation by Lings gives only half a sentence, whereas that particular verse consists of two complete sentences. The second quotation gives us one sentence, extracted from a verse containing four complete sentences. The complete verses are as follows:[13]

> And God's is the East and the West, so whither you turn thither is God's purpose. Surely God is Ample-giving, Knowing.
> And they say: God has taken to Himself a son – glory be to Him! Rather, whatever is in the heavens and the earth is His. All are obedient to Him.
> Wonderful Originator of the heavens and the earth! And when He decrees an affair, He says to it only, Be, and it is. (2:115-17)

> And call not with God any other god. There is no god but He. Everything will perish but He. His is the judgement, and to Him you will be brought back. (28:88)

> Every one on it passes away
> And there endures for ever the person of thy Lord, the Lord of glory and honour. (55:26, 27)

It is interesting that the Arabic word *Wajh* occurs in all these three instances. Muhammad Ali, on the authority of T. and L.L.,[14] explains the word as denoting 'countenance' or 'face', and also the 'course', 'purpose', 'object' or 'direction' one is pursuing. He adds that according to al-Raghib's *Dictionary of the Quran* this word 'signifies *attention* or *course*' (*The Holy Quran*, p. 51). Even if the word *Wajh* is taken in its primary sense of 'face' the term *wajhullah* or the 'face of god' can only be taken as a metaphorical or figurative (*mutashabih*) reference to the being of god. The interpretation of these verses presents no special difficulty:

(1) The first verse (2:115) refers, in order, to the following ideas: God's Supreme Transcendence and/or the Divine Authorship of the cosmos (His is the East and the West), Omnipresence (wherever you turn there is God), Providence (Ample-giving), and Omniscience (Knowing).

(2) 28.88. The ideas alluded to here are those of Divine Unity, Eternity, and Lordship of the universe – in relation to eschatology (God's judgement and man's return to Him).

(3) 55:26, 27. These two verses occur in the chapter entitled 'The Beneficent' (*Al-Rahman*), which speaks of God's universal Providence, and the constant refrain is, 'Which then of the bounties of your Lord will you deny?' The reference here is clearly to the contrast between the transient nature of the whole of the created order (all things pass away) as against the permanence of the Creator (God endures for ever). This straightforward way of understanding the Quran has the essential merit of being in perfect accord with its own fundamental categorial scheme.

We move on now to the second set of Lings's references to the Quran. He writes here of 'the Quranic doctrine of Nearness – Identity – Oneness', and we shall see how he arrives at it. First, there is the well-known verse about God's nearness to man: 'And certainly We created man, and We know what his mind suggests to him – and We are nearer to him than his life-vein' (50:16).

Lings quotes only the last part of this verse. He comments (p. 129):

In the following Holy Tradition[15] this nearness is expressed as identity: 'My slave seeketh unremittingly to draw nigh unto Me with devotions of his free will until I love him; and when I love him, I am the Hearing wherewith he heareth and the Sight wherewith he seeth and the Hand wherewith he smiteth and the Foot whereon he walketh.'

The proper procedure would be the exact reverse – the apparent 'identity' expressed in this Tradition must be set within the context of the Quran's fundamental categorial scheme, so that 'identity' must be understood in terms of the Quranic idea of God's *nearness*; in other words, it is a metaphorical expression of the degree of God's closeness to man. It is only by turning the universally recognised, and the only valid, method of interpreting a seemingly paradoxical Tradition (in the light of the plain Quranic teaching) on its head that Lings can speak of 'the Quranic doctrine of Nearness – Identity – Oneness'. He goes so far as to assert that this identity was already there, although it was not perceived as such by the mystic, and indeed the real agent of perception is God. In support of this he quotes the Quran (an incomplete verse). The entire verse reads:[16] 'No human vision can encompass Him, whereas He encompasses all human vision: for He alone is unfathomable, all-aware'

(6:103). This verse, read in its context, or even on its own, can clearly provide no such support. So there are, according to Lings, two levels of perception – the lower 'relative' one which turns out, at the higher level, to be 'pure illusion in the face of the Absolute Reality of his Presence'. These two levels are claimed to be referred to in the verse, 'We are nearer to him than ye are, although ye see not' (56:85) – a verse which, does not suggest anything beyond the nearness that we have already met with above. Lings adds that there cannot even be 'relative nearness' here, according to the verse quoted above (50:16), together with 8:24 (again he quotes only half a sentence). The whole verse reads: 'O you who believe! Respond to the call of God and the apostle whenever He calls you unto that which will give you life; and know that God intervenes between man and (the desires of) his heart, and that unto Him you shall be gathered'. Muhammad Asad comments, comprehensively, on this verse[17] as follows (*The Message of the Quran*, p. 242, no. 24):

> i.e., between a man's desires and the outward action that may result from those desires: indicating that God can turn man away from what his heart urges him to do (Raghib). In other words, it is God-consciousness alone that can prevent man from being misled by wrong desires and, thus, from becoming like 'those deaf, those dumb ones who do not use their reason' (verse 22 above); and it is God-consciousness alone that can enable man to follow the call 'unto that which gives life': that is, spiritual awareness of right and wrong and the will to act in accordance with this awareness.

Even if the verse is taken as a variation on the nearness theme, it only emphasises the degree of intimacy that is possible in the God-man relationship. Lings, however, maintains that 'the Oneness here expressed exceeds the Oneness of union'. Again, this is admissible only if 'exceeds the Oneness of Union' is a poetic way of expounding the Quranic doctrine of man's potentially extremely close relationship to God. But the distinction between God and man remains, and must always so remain.

Lings is of the view that some Quranic verses do not admit readily of any interpretation other than that in terms of the Oneness of Being doctrine. He includes the 'Nearness' verse among them; we have already found reason to reject this view. In addition, he mentions the verse 'He is the First and the Last and the Outwardly Manifest and the Inwardly Hidden' (57:3). So far from not allowing any other interpretation but that of Oneness of Being it is most easily understood as explained by the Prophet himself ('Sahih Muslim', 48:13, as quoted by Muhammad Ali, *The Holy Quran*, pp. 1028-9):

Thou art *the First*, so that there was nothing before Thee, and Thou art *the Last*, so that there is nothing after Thee, and Thou art *the Manifest*, or *the Ascendant* over all, so that there is nothing above Thee, and Thou art *the Hidden, the Knower* of the hidden things, so that there is nothing hidden from Thee.

Lings quotes the Tradition 'Thou art the Outwardly Manifest and there is nothing covering Thee' as a reference to the same doctrine; but this Tradition itself becomes clear when we juxtapose it to the Prophet's comment, on the Quran (57:3), that I have just quoted.

We are thus bound to conclude that the Quran and the Prophet's Traditions provide no warrant whatsoever for the Sufi doctrine of the Oneness of Being. Its origins must therefore be sought in extra-Islamic sources.[18]

9.2 (3)

Lings refers to Massignon's view that the doctrine was originally formulated by Ibn al-Arabi and concedes that the term *Wahdat al-Wujud* was perhaps not in general use before him. However, he insists that the doctrine itself is older than Ibn al-Arabi and, indeed, 'the more the question is studied the further it recedes along a purely Islamic line of descent'. This is already a highly provocative position and one that seems to be, particularly in view of our discussion of the Quran and *hadith*, both paradoxical as well as implausible. Lings proceeds boldly to call upon no less a person than al-Ghazali as a witness to his case. Now this is a move of considerable interest and significance – nothing could serve Lings's cause better than a successful attempt to buttress his very strained and heterodox interpretations of the Quran by invoking such a weighty authority and pellucid intellect. *But can he succeed*? The question suggests an answer of *a priori* kind.

We have already had occasion to refer to al-Ghazali's teaching on the Muslim doctrine of God (section 7.2). His formulation was seen as a perfectly orthodox exposition of the Quranic doctrine of the Supremely Transcendent Deity. It is highly improbable, and indeed quite incredible, that a thinker of his stature should eventually have made a complete *volte face* and espoused a doctrine of pantheistic monism. The matter is one of such gravity that any claim, or even suggestion, that he did so must be examined in the most scrupulously thorough manner possible.

Lings makes use specifically of two passages in al-Ghazali's *Mishkat al-Anwar* (*The Niche for Lights*). The first occurs in the context of the comment (examined above) that the Oneness of Being doctrine is only concerned with 'Absolute Reality', ordinary reality being labelled metaphorical (Lings, 1971, pp. 122-3 ff):

The Gnostics rise from the lowlands of metaphor to the peak of Verity; and at the fulfilment of their ascent they see directly face to face that there is naught in existence save only God and that everything perisheth but His Face, not simply that it perisheth at any given time but it hath never not perished . . . . Each thing hath two faces, a face of its own, and a face of its Lord; in respect of its own face it is nothingness, and in respect of the Face of God it is Being. Thus there is nothing in existence save only God and His Face, for everything perisheth but His Face, always and forever . . . so that the Gnostics need not wait for the Resurrection in order to hear the summons of the Creator proclaim: Unto whom this day is the Kingdom? Unto God, the One, the Irresistible, for this proclamation is eternally in their ears; nor do they understand from His Utterance God is Most Great (Allahu Akbar) that he is greater than others. God forbid! For there is nothing other than Himself in all existence, and therefore there is no term of comparison for His Greatness.

The second passage is quoted by way of countering Massignon's criticism of the doctrine on the ground that it denies the transcendence of God.

There is no he but He, for 'he' expresseth that unto which reference is made, and there can be no reference at all save only unto Him, for whenever thou makest a reference, that reference is unto Him even though thou knewest it not through thine ignorance of the Truth of Truths. . . . Thus 'there is no god but God' is the generality's proclamation of Unity, and 'there is no he but He' is that of the elect, for the former is more general, whereas the latter is more elect, more all-embracing, truer, more exact, and more operative in bringing him who useth it into the Presence of Unalloyed Singleness and Pure Oneness.

Both passages, in fact, occur close together in the text of the *Mishkat al-Anwar* (Gairdner, 1952, pp. 103-5, 112-13).

W. H. T. Gairdner, in the course of a perceptive introduction to his translation of the *Mishkat al-Anwar*, discusses the issue of whether or not al-Ghazali had succeeded 'in balancing himself upon the edge of the pantheistic abyss, and finding some foothold for his creationist theism, some position that cleared his conscience towards his orthodox co-religionists' (p. 61). His conclusion is that 'Ghazali himself contrived to use this ontology so as to *keep*, not lose, his hold on the reality and actuality of things, and that early training, central theological orthodoxy, and strong common sense proved by its help too strong for the pull towards pantheism' (p.67). His appraisal is based on a careful study of the internal evidence provided by al-Ghazali himself in the *Mishkat*.[19] A fundamental preliminary is the distinction between doctrine and experience: the all-important matter of their precise relationship will be considered later on. We must now examine the relevant parts of the *Mishkat* under these two separate headings.

Doctrine

At the level of doctrine there is good ground for holding that al-Ghazali did not in any way violate the Quran's fundamental categorial scheme.

(1) Consider first his ontology. Being, says al-Ghazali, is of two sorts: 'that which has being in itself, and that which derives its being from not-itself' (p. 103). The being of the latter is borrowed, and this is not real being; therefore it has being status only in relation to that which confers such status on it, and considered in itself it does not exist. Al-Ghazali then transposes this basic ontology into his theistic scheme. All things have two aspects or faces: one of its own and one in its relation to God. It is the latter (the God-aspect) which is being, so that god is the only truly existing Reality. Now a sort of God-world ontological continuity *can* be read into these ideas, but I submit that the following interpretation is more in keeping with the whole context of al-Ghazali's discussion. Essentially, al-Ghazali is not denying that the world is a real existent as ordinarily experienced. He is merely defining 'reality' in such a manner that the Supreme and Absolute Transcendence of God is preserved. In other words, if worldly things have been created by God they are, on *al-Ghazali's definition*, not truly real. However, it is important to see that the God-world (and God-man) ontological *duality* is maintained.

(2) This becomes clearer only a few lines later where al-Ghazali comments on the formula *Allahu Akbar* ('God is most great'). It is significant that he does so, as it were, at two levels. First, in terms of his ontology: 'All existence is exclusively His Aspect. Now it is impossible that He should be "greater" than His own Aspect.' However, at the second level (p. 105):

> The meaning is rather that He is too absolutely Great to be called
> Greater, or Most Great, by way of relation or comparison — too
> Great for anyone, whether Prophet or Angel, to grasp the real nature

of His Greatness. For none knows Allah with a real knowledge but He Himself; for every known falls necessarily under the sway and within the province of the Knower.

Here the categories 'anyone, whether Prophet or Angel', 'none' and 'every known' stand clearly opposed to, or contrasted with, the category of God.

Some further instances where the integrity of the Quran's fundamental categorial scheme is implicitly maintained are as follows.

(3) Al-Ghazali refers (p. 118) to two special categories of believers: the Saint-Friends of God who 'only see objects through and in Allah' (alluded to in the Quran 41:53), and the 'Learned', who 'first see objects and then see Allah in and through those objects' (Quran 3:6 and 41:53).

(4) The mystic, having progressed through the hierarchy of lights (stars, moon and sun) symbolising God's light, eventually turns to god: '*I have turned my face unto That Who made the heavens and the earth! I am a true believer, and not of those who associate other gods with Allah!*' (p. 128). Al-Ghazali explains the reference in 'That Who' as 'the vaguest kind of indication, destitute of all relation or comparison'; so much so, that 'this That' cannot be represented even by a symbol. 'Now He Who transcends all relations is ALLAH, the ONE REALITY.'

(5) The goal of the mystical quest is Allah – 'THE REAL EXISTENT', further characterised by al-Ghazali as 'an Existent who transcends ALL that is comprehensible by human Sight or human Insight; for they found IT transcendent of and separate from every characterization that in the foregoing we have made.' This last statement is decisive and should settle the matter of al-Ghazali's fundamentally orthodox position beyond doubt. It is significant that it occurs at the end of the *Mishkat* (p. 172). (It is very much to Gairdner's credit that this statement made a deep impression on him.)

Experience

We have already quoted (p. 75) the two passages from the *Mishkat* which Lings cites as evidence of al-Ghazali's adherence to the Oneness of Being doctrine. When these two passages are examined closely, *and especially in their own context*, it is clear that they refer primarily to *experiential* matters – specifically, the experiences of 'Allah's gnostics . . . *at the end of their Ascent*' (pp. 103, 104, my emphasis). These mystical experiences are reported on by the gnostics '*on their return* from their Ascent into the heaven of Reality' (p. 106, my emphasis). Further, al-Ghazali himself provides a very clear-headed and cogent analysis of such experience. This, unfortunately, is not the whole story – as he does confuse the issue somewhat by interpolations of a doctrinal kind. However, this should not obscure my initial point that what appear to be his extreme statements are no more than attempts to describe *what the mystic actually experiences* at the end of his spiritual journey.

Let us now follow the main lines of al-Ghazali's description and analysis of the Sufi experience of God. The truth of the Quranic verse *'everything perisheth except His Countenance, His Aspect'* (WAJH; 28: 88) is seen by the mystics 'at the end . . . as with the direct sight of eye-witnesses' (p. 104). (Here al-Ghazali explains the experience at length in terms of his basic ontology.) And further – 'these gnostics, on their return from their Ascent into the heaven of Reality, confess with one voice that they saw nought existent there save the One Real . . . the plurality of things fell away in its entirety. They were drowned in the absolute Unitude' (p. 106). Indicative of the extraordinary nature of the experience is the use of such phrases as 'their intelligences were lost in Its abyss', 'therein became they as dumbfounded things', 'drunken with a drunkenness wherein the sway of their own intelligence disappeared', and 'no capacity remained within them save to recall ALLAH' (p. 106). It was in such a state that the exclamations of 'I am The ONE REAL!' (Al-Hallaj) and 'Glory be to ME! How great is MY glory!' (Abu-Yazid al-Bistami) were made. These are the words of lovers who are 'passionate in their intoxication and ecstasy' (pp. 106, 107). *What, then, of the experience of 'identity'? Al-Ghazali's answer could not be plainer or more decisive* (p. 107):

> Then when that drunkenness abated and they came again under the sway of their intelligence, which is Allah's balance-scale upon earth, they knew that that had not been actual Identity, but only something resembling Identity; as in those words of the Lover at the height of his passion:
> 'I am He whom I love and He whom I love is I;
> We are two spirits immanent in one body.' (Al-Hallaj)

By way of further clarification al-Ghazali takes two examples. A man who has never seen a mirror in his life may, on first encountering one, mistake the image (in the mirror) for the form of the mirror itself. In other words, image and mirror are seen as one and the same thing. Another such person might mistake wine for the colour of the glass in which it is contained. Here there is a difference between saying, 'The wine *is* the wine-glass', and saying, ''tis *as though it were* the wine-glass'.

In the same way al-Ghazali's reformulation of the first part of the Muslim credo (There is no god but one God) as *'There is no he but HE'* is seen as 'more apt to give him who declares it entrance into the pure and absolute Oneness and Onliness'. This is 'the ultimate point of mortals' Ascent . . . when Plurality has been eliminated . . . . The upward Progress, The Ascent of the soul' (p. 113) then reaches its highest point. And again, at the end of the *Mishkat*, on the penultimate page, al-Ghazali states quite lucidly that 'the import of His word, *"All perisheth save His Countenance,"* becomes the experience of the soul' (p. 173).

On these grounds, therefore, we must reject Martin Lings's claim that al-Ghazali upheld the doctrine of the Oneness of Being. There has been some debate about the authenticity of this work (the *Mishkat*), largely on the grounds that al-Ghazali's views are extreme or heterodox (see Professor Montgomery Watt's balanced and scholarly appraisal in *The Encyclopaedia of Islam*.) Hopefully, my own analysis should contribute to this debate, at least indirectly, by showing that hasty judgment should not be passed on isolated bits quoted out of context.

9.2 (4)

This still leaves us, however, with the big question of the nature of mystical experience as distinct from its subsequent theoretical interpretation. Thus, quite apart from the doctrinal interpolations we have referred to in al-Ghazali, it is clear that even his claim that at the end of the spiritual quest the mystic experiences some kind of overwhelmingly intimate and intense 'identification' with God involves interpretation of a complex and elaborate kind – specifically in terms of Muslim theism. This is clearly an important issue and I will now return to Martin Lings to show that his failure to make the distinction between *experience* and *interpretation* is the source of a serious confusion between the goal of the mystical quest and the doctrine in terms of which that goal is anticipated or envisaged.

Lings writes: 'this doctrine is necessarily present whenever there is explicit reference to the Supreme Truth', so that, if the Supreme Truth is allowed to fade away into the background, then, correspondingly, this doctrine will also fade out – *'since apart from the Infinite and Eternal Present it is meaningless'* (p. 124, my emphasis). These last quoted words are most significant – they clearly imply that the truth or validity of the doctrine of Oneness of Being cannot be established apart from the actual experience of the mystic. This interpretation is strengthened by the whole context of Lings's discussion, where he relates the doctrine to the actual meditative (*dhikr*) practice of the Sufis. He emphasises that in mysticism there is 'a continual shifting of the centre of consciousness from one plane to another'. Thus, the novice in the *Alawi Tariqah* (order) has to replace 'much of the agility of "profane intelligence"' with 'an agility of a different order, comparable to that of a bird which continually changes the level of its flight'. The mystic quest has a beginning and an End, and the transitional stages in between are of 'distinct levels of intelligence' or of 'different levels of thought'. 'It follows that the formulations of any one mystic are unlikely to be all from the same standpoint.' In other words, the doctrinal formulations of the Sufis will depend upon the particular nature of the individual's mystical experience. Lings adds the following (in a footnote): 'the refusal to see that mysticism is never a "system" and that mystics are consciously and methodically "inconsistent", taking now one standpoint, now another, has led to much confusion, especially as regards *Wahdat al-Wujud*.' Now the upshot of all this is that the doctrine of Oneness of Being is held to be a matter of mystical experience – its truth is manifested to the mystic at the end of his spiritual voyage.[20] The following passage states this idea clearly and forcefully (pp. 124–6):

> But it is natural that spiritual Masters should stress *Wahdat al-Wujud* above all, because it is the Supreme Truth and therefore the ultimate goal of all mysticism ... relentless insistence upon the doctrine has therefore a great methodic, not to say 'hypnotic', value, for it helps the disciple to place himself virtually in the Eternal Present when he cannot do so actually.

This conclusion must be rejected without compunction. In fact, Lings's discussion contains seeds, which, if allowed to germinate, would undermine it. If the *doctrinal* formulations of the Sufis are related to the particular nature of their experiences then quite clearly the way is open, at the very least, to theological disorientation and, at worst, to doctrinal chaos. There is, in fact, a serious *logical* confusion here: a doctrine is not the kind of 'thing' which can be 'given' as it were, in any kind of experience, mystical or otherwise. It may be that a particular theological doctrine is held to be vindicated by a particular mystical experience, or that, more plausibly, a specific mystical experience is *interpreted* in terms of a specific theological doctrine, but this is an entirely different matter. This consideration brings to a head the whole question of *experience* and *interpretation* in mysticism. A consideration of the issues involved in this question (mystical experience and its interpretation) will enable us to return to the Sufi doctrine of Oneness of Being more fruitfully, and hopefully to suggest a definitive clarification of some essential issues.

Chapter 10

Mystical experience and interpretation

10.1 W. T. Stace

As a preliminary to this question I would draw attention to the important paper 'Definitions of mysticism' by E. G. Parrinder, already referred to earlier (section 9.2). It is a balanced and scholarly overall discussion and summary, and brings out pointedly the acute difficulties posed by attempts to define and classify mystical experience.

The notion of 'experience and interpretation' in mysticism has been clearly and firmly expounded by W. T. Stace (*Mysticism and Philosophy*, ch. 1.5). His views have been criticised and do stand in need of some modification and refinement, but their central insight seems to me to be unassailable. Therefore they provide a solid base, as well as a convenient point of departure, for our present discussion.

Stace makes a distinction between mystical experience and its conceptual interpretation, and argues that this is analogous to the distinction between sense experience and its interpretation: 'I use the word "interpretation" to mean anything which the conceptual intellect adds to the experience . . . classificatory concepts, or a logical inference, or an explanatory hypothesis.' He gives the neat example of the American visitor who tried to shake hands with a waxwork policeman at the entrance of Madame Tussaud's in London. Stace infers from this that the visitor initially misinterpreted his sense experience (as a live policeman) and subsequently interpreted it correctly (as a wax figure). He concludes that as there were two interpretations of one experience it proves the distinguishability of an interpretation from an experience.

Stace argues that a parallel distinction must be made between mystical experience and its interpretation, although he does allow for the much greater difficulty here in deciding exactly what part of a mystic's account

should be taken as strictly descriptive of the experie
part constitutes his interpretation. But he insists tha
vitally important, and for two reasons. First, althoug.
ence, if isolable, would be indubitable, any interpret
mistakes. Second, it has often been argued that all mysi
are basically the same in all ages and cultures; Stace ad.
an extremely difficult question. Thus, for instance, Chrisi
mystics base very different beliefs on their respective exp ـᴗ.ᴗces. This
can be explained either on the hypothesis that the experiences, although
mystical in both cases, are basically different, or on the hypothesis that
the experience is basically the same but that each puts a different intellectual interpretation upon it – the interpretation being derived, of
course, from the mystic's own religious culture.

Stace argues that Professor R. C. Zaehner (in his book *Mysticism:
Sacred and Profane*) is gravely misled by his failure to make a clear distinction between experience and interpretation. The specific example
which Stace considers here adds greatly, in my view, to the clarity,
force and cogency of his thesis. He refers to the frequent descriptions in
the records of introvertive mysticism, of 'the experience of an absolute
undifferentiated and distinctionless unity'. This experience is described
by Christian mystics such as Eckhart and Ruysbroeck, and by the
ancient Hindu mystics who composed the *Upanishads* in almost identical
terms. Yet Professor Zaehner insists that the experiences must have
been different because the Christians and the Hindus in question were
led to different doctrinal positions (orthodox trinitarian theology and
Hindu pantheism). He does not consider the alternative hypothesis that
a different interpretation is being put in each case upon a fundamentally
identical experience. Stace argues: 'But the point is that Professor
Zaehner's conclusion simply does not follow from the mere fact that
the *beliefs* which Christian mystics based upon their experiences are different from the *beliefs* which the Indians based on theirs' (p. 36). He
concludes that a proper and fair assessment of the two possible hypo-
theses requires a genuine grasp of the distinction between experience
and interpretation.

Subsequently Stace undertakes an extended consideration (especially
chapters 2 and 4) of the records of mystics all over the world, and in all
ages and cultures. He comes to the conclusion that the actual experience
is identical (introvertive mysticism) but that various distinct interpretations are put on it according to the prevailing religious, cultural and
historical pressures. It is the supreme merit of Stace's very thorough and
elaborate survey that the actual descriptive records are subjected to

ute scrutiny. Here I cannot agree with J.N. Findlay's assertion (*Ascent to the Absolute*, ch. 10) that Stace's account is deeply faulty, being merely 'external and empirical'. Indeed, Findlay's own thesis that mysticism is more deeply revelatory of the nature and being of the world is only a somewhat grandiose and rhetorical extension of any one of numerous statements made by Stace about the significance of the unitary consciousness (introvertive) and the unifying vision (extrovertive) for the experiencing mystic.[1]

Stace's account includes the very sound and useful idea of varying *levels of interpretation* of mystical experience. This is again parallel to the case of sense experience; for instance, seeing a red colour involves a low-level interpretation, whereas the physicist's account of colours in terms of the wave theory of light is a very high-level interpretation. Essentially the same idea has been developed somewhat further by Ninian Smart who writes of 'the degree of ramification' of the concepts used in interpretation ('Interpretation and mystical experience'). He gives the neat example of Suso's statement, 'in this merging of itself in God the spirit passes away' (p. 79). Here the degree of ramification decreases progressively as we go from the concept 'God' to the concept 'spirit', and thence to the concept 'pass away'.

10.2 Bruce Garside's critique of Stace

From the opposite side — that of those, such as Rudolf Otto and R. C. Zaehner, who hold that mystical experiences are essentially different — Stace has been criticised, largely unfairly, by Bruce Garside ('Language and the interpretation of mystical experience'). Garside regards Stace's example of the waxwork policeman as rather misleading since it does not involve what is usually called 'interpreting'; the American saw the figure *as* a live policeman, but this involves an entirely different analysis. Now we may concede the point to Garside that Stace's analysis, *as thus stated*, *is* somewhat vulnerable. However, this does *not* affect the soundness of the main insight which he is trying to express — namely, that sense experience is one thing and its conceptual interpretation quite another. It is easily shown that a slight refinement of Stace's analysis is all that is needed to apply the experience/interpretation schema to his chosen example in a concrete and meaningful way. Equally, such a refinement would show that Garside's argument — that the American's seeing the wax figure *as* a live policeman involves an entirely different analysis — does not necessarily follow. Let us reconsider Stace's example.

The American visitor 'had a sense-experience which he first wrongly interpreted as a live policeman and later interpreted correctly as a wax figure'. Now it is important here to be quite clear about the notion of interpretation – and, indeed, this is the key to the whole analysis. Two things are needed for interpretation to occur: a primary set of data which is then subjected to a *conscious* and *deliberate* process of working out so that some higher thought structure or configuration results. The primary set of data in Stace's example comprises all the various coloured shapes and surfaces, etc., which make up the wax figure. The process of interpretation (say, in the visitor's head) would proceed thus: 'Now I wonder if this is a live policeman?' So a problem is posed, and the visitor 'works out' the result as follows: 'The colour and texture of the hands are somewhat waxen, and this does not look like real skin. But the eyes are so real', and so forth. All the data of sense experience are subjected in this way to a process of scrutiny and interpretation, and, in the end, the visitor says, 'Well, I think this *is* a live policeman'. Here, therefore, a conscious process of interpretation supervenes upon the more prior awareness of an assemblage of sensory data. When the visitor actually tries to shake hands a fresh set of data enables him to make the right interpretation – i.e., of his sensory experience – as a wax figure. The following example should make this clearer; this is a highly simplified and schematised account. Two visitors to London, both only slightly familiar with the capital, drive in together on a foggy winter's night. They have lost their way. Presently they see an illuminated area in the distance and one of them says, 'I think we are approaching Piccadilly Circus', but his friend disagrees: 'No, I think it looks like Trafalgar Square.' Now clearly the actual details of the sensory experience are the same in the two cases – 'that bright spot, those dark shapes, the bluish line', and so on. So long as the two visitors are confined to a bare description at this level they will, allowing for minor differences in perspective and visual acuity, obviously agree. But beyond this description, each visitor *interprets* the data according to what he thinks he is seeing, guided perhaps by recollections of past visits to London, photographs and the like. So that 'that bright spot' might be interpreted as a particular monument, 'those dark shapes' as famous buildings, and so on. So here we have a clear, and clearly distinguishable, example of experience and interpretation.

Garside asserts that the statement that '*x* is seen as *y*' involves some analysis entirely different from that required by the notion of interpretation. This is demonstrably false, for it makes perfectly good sense to elaborate on the statement that the American visitor saw the wax figure *as* a live policeman in such terms as I have sketched out in my more refined account of the same situation above. '*x* is seen as *y*' is in fact a *generic* statement, for if we ask 'How does this come about?' the following *specific* explanations may legitimately be given:

(a) It was simply a mistake (of some sort).
(b) It was an optical illusion.
(c) It was a question of interpretation.

And so we can go on adding to this list.

Garside attributes Stace's alleged mis-description of the American visitor's experience at Madame Tussaud's to his 'failure to realise that what he calls an interpretative framework and I have referred to as a "set" enters into the experience itself as a constitutive factor'. It is therefore inevitable that the experiences of people in different religious traditions should be different, and so it is senseless to look for 'an "authentic" description of a mystical experience "undistorted" by any interpretative framework'. Finally, he claims that the supposedly neutral description culled by Stace from different traditions 'turns out to be expressed in language associated with the metaphysics of Hegel'. Let us take these criticisms in order.

We have already seen that Stace's account, as refined, is not a mis-description. So, far from failing to realise that interpretation is an essential ingredient of all experience, Stace emphasises this point (pp. 31-2). Immediately after introducing his notion of experience and interpretation (in mysticism as well as in ordinary sense experience) he writes: 'it is probably impossible in both cases to isolate "pure" experience', so that these two things 'are distinguishable though not completely separable'. Stace, indeed, goes so far as to allow 'even that such a pure experience is psychologically impossible'. Reverting to his example of the wax figure, Stace argues that it was recognised from the outset that it was a material thing of some sort (having some kind of colour and the shape of a human being), 'And since this involved the application of classificatory concepts to the sensations, there was from the first some degree of interpretation'. It is on such a basis that Stace is able to claim further that although this experience/interpretation distinction is a rough one it is almost indispensable in the practical business of everyday living. Now while there are no grounds here for criticising Stace on the lines suggested by Garside, this does not mean that they are in fact in agreement. Before this can be brought out clearly, Stace's view must be subjected here to a little more refinement.

We have already noted that the two essential factors needed for interpretation to occur are (1) the existence of a primary set of data and (2) a conscious process of scrutiny, analysis, inference, etc., which yields a higher-order thought structure – the interpretation. Now, strictly speaking, the sort of process which Stace has described as 'the application of classificatory concepts to the sensations' is a *prerequisite* for inter-pretation, but does not, in itself, constitute 'interpretation'. Schemati-cally, I propose the following simple model for the understanding of what actually goes on.

(1) There is the actual fabric of 'our experience of the world' – whose texture is of the most subtle and delicate kind, ever-flowing, and infinitely variegated.
(2) This raw 'stuff' of experience – *viz*. (1) – is then progressively organised, classified and labelled in simple and complex ways. This gives us a definite picture of the world – a world of colours and sounds (seen and heard), anxieties and pains (felt), ideas and numbers (thought), mermaids and castles-in-the-air (imagined), and so on.
(3) It is this sort of primary data – *viz*. (2) – which is subjected to the more elaborate process of *interpretation*.[2]

Now what Stace insistently, and quite rightly, calls *descriptions* of mystical experience are in fact based on, or at least assume, something like stage (2) of this schema. Take the following two examples:

(1) From the *Mandukya Upanishad*: 'It is pure unitary consciousness wherein awareness of the world and of multiplicity is completely ob-literated. It is ineffable peace' (Stace, p. 88).
(2) From the mediaeval Catholic mystic Ruysbroeck: 'There he finds revealed an Eternal Light . . . . It (his spirit) is undifferentiated and without distinction, and therefore it feels nothing but the unity' (p. 94).

As Stace remarks: 'the two experiences recorded, one of the Hindu, the other of the Catholic Christian, are identical point by point.' Yet the Hindu *interpretation* of the experience is that it establishes *the identity of the individual self with the Universal Self*, whereas the Chris-tian *interpretation* is that the experience involves *union with God*. Stace illustrates his point with a great wealth of examples from all of the world's major religious traditions. The distinction between experience and inter-pretation (seen neatly in the simple example just quoted) is brought out very clearly and vigorously by his examples and comments. As against this approach the 'critical' statements made by Garside must be dismissed as high-handed and irresponsible allegations. Indeed, Garside does not either attempt a fresh analysis of any of Stace's examples, or offer any illustrations of his own — this is in keeping with his quite *a priori* and dogmatic approach. And his comment that Stace's supposedly neutral description 'turns out to be expressed in language associated with the metaphysics of Hegel' either betrays an abysmal ignorance of Hegel or is simply disingenuous nonsense. A final word about Garside. He bases his whole discussion on a 'general model of experience' which is derived from the crude epistemological assumptions of certain positivistically inclined branches of psychology. His claim that 'the model is of Kantian inspiration' only compounds simple-mindedness with incoherence.

10.3 Pantheism

The distinction between experience and interpretation in relation to mystical experience has thus been firmly established. We are now ready to consider the question of pantheism, and this discussion will highlight the experience/interpretation schema, and demonstrate both its soundness and value. It is extremely instructive here to take some of the main points in Stace's own discussion of pantheism (ch. 4).

Stace prefaces his discussion of pantheism with the following remark: 'We can never say that any of our conclusions on the philosophical implications of mysticism are more than what seem to us, after careful and impartial sifting of the evidence, the most probable among possible rival views' (p. 207). This is most creditable. With this proviso Stace concludes that mystical experience is not merely subjective, 'but is in very truth what the mystics themselves claim, namely a direct experience of the One, the Universal Self, God'. We can agree with this conclusion *provisionally*. This agreement must remain tentative as the precise sense of the phrase 'a direct experience of . . . God' will emerge only when we consider (in part III) the *logical* status of 'God'.

Pantheism has been defined in various ways.[3] Stace attempts to re-define it in a manner which he believes to be more profound than the usual conceptions. His definition is the simultaneous assertion of the two propositions that the world *is*, as well as *is not*, identical with God. Now, we need not consider this re-definition as it is not relevant to the substance of our inquiry. Stace also introduces the useful notion of 'mystical idea': this is roughly the same as an interpretation. The 'idea' is an interpretation of an actual mystical experience. But then he adds that, 'It is a transcription of certain characteristics of mystical experience' (p. 38). This last statement is rather misleading, and is also incon-

sistent with the earlier proposition that a mystical idea involves interpretation; this difficulty will become clearer when we examine Stace's
argument in more detail. He gives pantheism as an example of a mystical idea. Indeed, Stace emphasises that although pantheism may wear
the external dress of reason and argument, its psychological origins are
always in actual mystical experience.[4]

This brings us to *the* crucial question about pantheism, and we must
note carefully Stace's own formulation of it: 'Thus the significant question about pantheism is not whether the arguments for it are good logic
but whether it is the correct interpretation of mystical experience. This
is the problem now before us' (pp. 218-19). We have already observed
that interpretation involves a conscious process of 'working out' on the
basis of a set of given data. The resulting higher thought structure is the
actual theory or doctrine in terms of which the data are held to have
been interpreted. So an important question now arises: Where does the
theory or doctrine come from? The phrase 'the resulting higher thought
structure' might suggest that it is in some sense inferred or derived from
the actual experience but this is demonstrably not the case. A parallel
from the discipline of history is helpful here. Consider the case of a
Marxist historian who is faced with the question of interpreting a given
set of data — say, the social and political factors implicated in a time of
revolutionary upheaval. He utilises such notions as those of 'the struggle
of the classes', 'the contradictions of capitalism', 'the economic infra-
structure', and so forth in order to interpret the given data. Now it is
clearly *not* the case that such elaborate theoretical notions are arrived
at by a straightforward process of inference or description on the basis
of the given data. Otherwise the same data could not, in principle, be
interpreted in terms of a variety of non-Marxist positions. So the conclusion must be that the theory in terms of which an interpretation is
effected must have some source quite apart from the data it is brought
to bear upon. In other words, like the data, it is in some sense 'given'.
Similar parallels could be drawn from the fields of aesthetics, or of
natural science. As long as we can maintain this distinction between
data and *theory* we need not, at this stage, inquire further into either
their precise relationship or the actual source of the latter. Stace freely
acknowledges that pantheism is a philosophical theory (e.g., pp. 218,
234) but he puts his emphasis on the fact that its roots are mystical.
Clearly there is a big problem here: How do mystics arrive at such a
sophisticated theory on the basis of their experiences? Stace himself
points out that mystics are, as a rule, not philosophers or metaphysicians.
In fact, 'the mystic as such is not a theorist, nor interested in theory —

with a few great exceptions such as Eckhart, Plotinus, and the Buddha' (p. 234).[5] This caveat only increases the difficulty further.

In his section on the 'Justification of Pantheism' (ch. 4.5) Stace considers an actual example of a record of the introvertive type of mystical experience. He starts from the experience of 'pure consciousness' – variously interpreted, e.g., as God (the theistic religions), *Brahman-Atman* (Upanishadic Hinduism), the Void (Buddhism). The next step in his argument is the attempt to show that this experience also yields 'the absolute infinite'. Stace quotes the reference to Brahman in the *Mandukya Upanishad* as 'beyond relation, featureless, unthinkable. in which all is still', and comments: 'This thought is not an isolated *aperçu* but is constantly reiterated in different forms in the Upanishads. It must not be mistaken for the conclusion of some metaphysical chain of argument. It is a direct report of immediate experience' (pp. 240-1). This 'Absolute', argues Stace, differs from the Absolutes of Hegel or Bradley since the authors of the Upanishads were seers and not philosophers. 'And they reported that what they had seen was "beyond relation, featureless, unthinkable, in which all is still."' At this point Stace commences, quite unwittingly, *a complex process of interpretation and theory construction*. The first move in this process is the assertion that 'But that which is totally beyond all relations is necessarily infinite. For the infinite is that which is not limited by anything else.' Now this is clearly already a *theoretical* matter – it amounts to a specific definition of the notion of 'the infinite'. Further, it is, arguably, an inadequate definition – but I let that pass now. Stace elaborates on his definition as follows. The word 'infinite' has only two intelligible senses – one is the mathematical sense (the endlessness of a series of items), and the other sense is that conveyed by the word in the Upanishads and in Spinoza. He quotes the *Chandogya Upanishad*: 'Where one sees nothing else, hears nothing else, understands nothing else, that is the Infinite. Where one sees something else, hears something else, understands something else, that is the finite.' He comments as follows: 'In other words the infinite is that outside which, and other than which, there is nothing. This is the same conception of the infinite as that which is given in Spinoza's definition of Substance.' He then discusses Spinoza's definition of 'Substance' briefly. Stace concludes, somewhat dogmatically, with the following set of related propositions (which I set out numerically):

(1) God's infinity cannot be of the mathematical kind. Therefore it must be the infinity in the Upanishadic and Spinozistic sense.
(2) The infinite in this sense is 'that outside which, and other than

which, there is nothing'. Therefore there is nothing other than God. (3) From this it follows that 'the world cannot be other than, or fall outside of, God'.

Now clearly we can question every stage of this argument – but that is beside my central concern here. What I rather wish to emphasise here is the yawning gap between the straightforward characterisation of mystical experience as 'beyond relation, featureless, unthinkable, in which all is still' and this kind of elaborate theory construction. The former is merely a descriptive account of whatever constitutes the phenomenology of mystical experience, whereas the latter implies a sophisticated process of intellective, discursive reasoning. In a word, this is the gap between *experience* and *theory*. Stace writes: 'This is the source of the pantheism of the Upanishads as well as of Spinoza' but this particular source is *not* a datum of experience – it is, in fact, a matter of philosophical, or, more precisely, logical and metaphysical reasoning. So Stace's argument at this point is entirely self-contradictory – for he starts from the thesis that 'the infinite' is given in 'a direct report of immediate experience'. He further asserts that, 'It explains precisely the relation between mystical experience and pantheism which has been mentioned before only in vague terms.' But this 'explanation' is no more than a tautology: mystical experience is actually *interpreted* in terms of this theory (pantheism). Stace goes on: 'We see therefore that pantheism is forced upon us by mysticism together with a proper understanding of the meaning of the notion of the infinite.' So a *dual* origin is now being posited for pantheism: (1) It is 'forced upon us by mysticism'. (Stace's argument is circular: (a) mysticism leads to pantheism, and (b) pantheism provides the interpretation of mystical experience.) (2) It is derived from the idea of 'the infinite'. Thus, Stace's whole case is incoherent as well as inconsistent – he has flouted his own fundamental premise of the distinction between experience and interpretation. We must therefore firmly and decisively reject his conclusion that 'pantheism is not a merely remote intellectual theory based upon experience, but a direct transcript of the experience itself' (p. 246).

The correct analysis would appear to be as follows. Pantheism is a high-level metaphysical theory whose sources lie in philosophical inquiry and speculation. The theory is then used in the interpretation of mystical experience. This raises complex issues of a logical and epistemological kind. For instance, the question of the truth of pantheism cannot be easily settled. Thus, while it can be conceded that mystical experience may be held, *in some sense*, to '*correspond*' to this theory it cannot, in itself, provide evidence of its truth. A valid *a priori* approach to the question of truth would consist in the scrutiny of both the general philosophical premises as well as the specific arguments on which it is based. The evidence from the whole range of our ordinary experience of the world, scientific knowledge, theological doctrine, moral and religious experience would clearly also be relevant (but this raises matters outside the scope of the present work).

We are left, then, with the all-important distinction between mystical experience and its conceptual interpretation − a distinction which Stace himself made with force and clarity at the very beginning of his inquiry. We can now return to our discussion of the Sufi doctrine of Oneness of Being. In our conclusion there (9.2(4)) it was noted that Martin Lings's idea that *Wahdat al-Wujud* constituted 'the ultimate goal of all mysticism' involved a serious *logical* error, since 'a doctrine is not the kind of "thing" which can be "given" as it were, in any kind of experience, mystical or otherwise'. We have found Stace making a similar, or at least related, mistake − this was seen clearly in his discussion of pantheism. Both authors have, in fact, committed the kind of logical error usually described as a category mistake. Thus, although we may concede that the Sufi experience has been *interpreted* at various times in terms of the *Wahdat al-Wujud* doctrine, we cannot appeal to such experience as a proof of its truth.

Part III

Beyond Iqbal: the nature of the problem of God

From the beginning of the *Quran* to the end, 'Tis wholly concerned with the abandonment of secondary causes and means. And now farewell to this subject.

The explanation of the mystery thereof is not given by the meddlesome intellect: do service to God, in order that it may become clear to you.

The philosopher is in bondage to things perceived by the intellect; but the pure saint is he that rides as a prince on the Intellect of intellect.

From the *Mathnawi of Jalaluddin Rumi*

Chapter 11

The logic of the infinite

11.1

In the latter part of chapter 1 of *The Reconstruction* ('Knowledge and religious experience') Iqbal makes some 'general observations on the main characteristics of mystic experience' (p. 18). His very first point is that 'we know God just as we know other objects', and he bases this thesis on the analogy he sees between ordinary sense experience and mystical experience. Thus, Iqbal argues that just as 'our knowledge of the external world' is derived from the 'interpretation of sense-data' so also 'our knowledge of God' is arrived at by an interpretation of mystical experience. However, he does not say what this process of 'interpretation' involves. Presumably this knowledge of God would link up with the 'knowledge of God's behaviour' constituted by the knowledge of nature (*The Reconstruction*, ch. II). Both positions are, perhaps arguably, implied by, or at least consistent with, the fact that Iqbal has developed a *finite* concept of God. But they are not, as stated by Iqbal, consistent with the Quranic doctrine of God's supreme transcendence and his immanence (he is very close to man, etc.). Iqbal's position is, in fact, more complicated. In chapter I he also asserts that 'the mystic state is a moment of intimate association with a unique other Self, *transcending*, encompassing, and momentarily suppressing the private personality of the subject of experience' (p. 19). And again in chapter II – nature is 'a living ever-growing organism whose growth has no final external limits. Its only limit is internal, i.e. the *immanent* self which animates and sustains the whole' (p. 56). I have emphasised the terms 'transcending' and 'immanent' in these two quotations. Is this perhaps a concession to the Quranic doctrine of God? If so, it would undermine the general line of Iqbal's argument. In any case, this reference to Iqbal serves to show the difficulty, and perhaps ambiguity, in the notions of transcendence and immanence.

These two terms are of wide currency, and a fairly standard way of stating an important truth (it is often assumed) is the statement: *God is transcendent, but also immanent.* What do these terms mean? This is a muddled area, and a convenient point of entry into it is provided by Ninian Smart's brief discussion in his recent book *The Concept of Worship.* He writes: 'The main sense that one can give to the thought that God has a place in some sense "beyond" the cosmos is that he exists, without spatial predicates attaching to him, in such a way that he is different from the cosmos and "behind" it' (p. 39) – the 'behind' and the 'beyond' are, of course, spatial analogies. Then there is the contrast between the immanent ('God's working in the world, e.g. through his preserving power, providentiality and so on') and the transcendent. He argues that this distinction cannot be maintained for (p. 40):

> When you say that God is in all things and when you say that God is beyond or behind all things, you appear to be saying two different things; but how can you be, considering that 'in', 'behind' and 'beyond' are analogical, not literal? And how can one aver that the differing analogical directions do not amount to the same direction?

Smart then considers God's 'continuous creation of the world ... working thus in all things'. He calls this 'omnipresence', and equates it with immanence. This is a confused discussion, and it helps to underline the fact that these terms need extremely delicate handling. The source of the confusion lies in the *apparently* correlative character of the transcendence/immanence polarity. The correlativity is, in fact, only *verbal.* Strictly speaking, the two concepts of transcendence and immanence answer two entirely distinct questions, respectively of the kind: *What?* and *Where?* More fully, the first question ought to be phrased: What is the nature of God? and the second one: Where is God? The answer to the first question is a negative one – He is not like anything in the world. The second question is answered, paradoxically, thus: He is everywhere, i.e. in the sense of His omnipresence. Smart is therefore mistaken in interpreting the term transcendence in the sense of various spatial analogies. This becomes very clear when we consider the dictionary meaning of the word:

> (1) (Especially of God) existing apart from, not subject to limitations of, the material universe (*Concise Oxford English Dictionary*).
> (2) Of the Deity: In His being, exalted above and distinct from the universe (*Shorter Oxford English Dictionary*).

Now clearly the sense conveyed by these two definitions is that of 'other than the world'. On the other hand, immanence means 'in the world'. More fully, and precisely, the nature of God is *wholly other than* anything worldly (He is transcendent), but he is *present everywhere* in the world (He is immanent). Now the concept of God's transcendence is closely related to that of His *infinity*, for if it is the case that God's being is *'wholly other than'* the world it goes necessarily beyond the *finite* sphere. This is already clear from the dictionary definition of the word transcendent: God is 'exalted above and distinct from the universe'; He is 'not subject to limitations of the material universe'. What, then, is the sense of the *'infinite'*? This brings us to the heart of the *logical* problem involved in the question of 'God'.

A finite God is something clearly intelligible, and comprehensible – for instance, the God of Whitehead (and Hartshorne), and Iqbal. H. P. Owen has argued (*Concepts of Deity*) that a finite God is developed in order to complete a metaphysical system, and it therefore differs from the God of revelation. Thus the finite God is the God, *par excellence*, of speculative philosophy, whereas the God of religion is truly 'the Infinite'. Rudolf Otto's *sensus numinis* is the result of the living, experiential encounter of man with the God of religion.

The central, and peculiar, *logical* problem involved in the notion of an infinite God emerges when we consider a traditional statement about it such as, for instance, that made by H. P. Owen (*op. cit.*, p. 53):

> Although the idea of an infinite God does not give rational satisfaction in the sense that it permits us to comprehend his nature, it alone makes the existence of both the world and him finally intelligible. Furthermore, although an infinite God wholly transcends our understanding, the idea of him is not self-contradictory. Nor are we left without any positive knowledge of him.

This is an internally incoherent statement; specifically, there are two major inconsistencies: (1) if we cannot comprehend the nature of an infinite God it follows, as a matter of logical necessity, that His existence cannot be intelligible; (2) if an infinite God *'wholly transcends our understanding'* then we cannot have any idea of Him and, even less, any positive knowledge of Him. The position of H. D. Lewis is an advance on this; he writes of (*Philosophy of Religion*, p. 141):[1]

> the absolute character of the mystery involved [and (p. 155):] of the inevitability of there being the completion which finite thought lacks .... There can be no means therefore of determining what it is to be God. We have not even a partial reduction of that mystery. The nature of God is in this sense altogether hidden.

However, Lewis does not take his position to its logical conclusion, as evidenced by such statements as (pp. 144, 152, 154, 155):

a Reality which is complete and self-contained

God is 'a unique Reality which falls altogether outside ordinary discourse. What holds without exception of finite things does not hold of God; He is the supreme exception, just because He is God.

It is not that our thought here is empty or without content, it is the richest thought of all, but from the nature of the case we cannot make it more explicit than the affirmation of there having to be Supreme or Ultimate Being. That is all we know directly of God.

Now it is clear that these statements contain the sort of tension and incoherence just noted in the case of H. P. Owen, and, more importantly, they cannot be reconciled with Lewis's own fundamental premise – as quoted above. This brings us to the crux of the matter – logical purity demands that it is impossible to specify the nature of the referent in the term 'the infinite', for, as we have just seen, any attempt, however subtle or carefully qualified, to 'fill out' the character of the 'object' in question will, *ipso facto*, render it *finite*. In other words the term 'the infinite' must be allowed to possess this peculiar logical property that it – a finite term – constitutes a meaningful but paradoxical attempt to refer to some 'object' or 'sphere' outside the finite one.[2] It follows therefore that the terms finite and infinite, when used in the universe of discourse about God, are *not* correlative – or, more precisely, they are not logically equivalent. The final upshot of this discussion is this: the term 'the infinite' is at the intersection of two distinct universes of discourse. In one of these, finite/infinite are correlative (i.e., logically continuous) terms – in the other they are not: being logically discontinuous or disjunct. 'The other' is of course itself a paradoxical reference, since the phrase 'the other, distinct, universe of discourse' can convey a definite and precise meaning only in terms of the ordinary, finite universe of discourse. This attempt to specify as precisely as possible the logical peculiarities and properties of the term 'the infinite' has quite far-reaching implications – for instance, many traditional ways of approaching the problem of God are ruled out *in principle*. We consider a few examples now.

11.2 Analogy

In an exceptionally penetrating argument, James F. Ross[3] has recently attempted 'to restate the analogy theory of St. Thomas Aquinas in terms of modern semantic analysis'. He goes on to consider its philosophical and historical significance (p. 93):

It is essentially a reply to the question: 'Can you show that theological statements are meaningful? A. N. Prior has remarked: 'The real intellectual difficulty of the believer or would-be believer is not the problem of proof but the problem of meaning.'

He considers the interpretations of authors like Flew and MacKinnon, Farrer, and Mascall 'seriously deficient and misleading, and I shall endeavour to show implicitly both how little they understood the complexity of the doctrine and how much more penetrating a language theory the analogy rules constitute than most modern writers have supposed' (p. 94). His argument is close, subtle, and lengthy. However, it is my considered view that Ross, his intricate semantic analysis notwithstanding, does not succeed. I can only state my conclusion here in a somewhat schematic, and also dogmatic, manner. The pivotal point of my objection is that Ross has not grasped the logic of the infinite properly. The application of the analogy rules to God-language turns on 'the similarity between God and creatures', for 'Aquinas is not committed to the absurd notion that God is entirely different from creatures'. Hence if G-statement predicates (with God or a synonym as subject) are *totally equivocal* with respect to the corresponding E-statement predicates (with objects of ordinary experience as subject) then all G-statements are meaningless. Again, if G-statement predicates are *univocal* with respect to the corresponding E-statement predicates, then God will be anthropomorphic (a basic assumption being that our descriptive categories are necessarily homocentric). Hence Aquinas distinguishes the *modus significandi* from the *res significata*: 'part of the meaning of the predicate terms is the *mode* of existence of the entity to which the property is attributed'. This leads to the conclusion that the G-statement predicates are *partially equivocal* with respect to their E-statement counterparts. In this way Aquinas builds a sort of logical bridge between man and God. Its central, and decisive, weakness is that it is based on the logical assumption that a *finite component* is shared by man and God. But this is inadmissible from the viewpoint of the logic of the infinite we have attempted to sketch out, for if this particular point be conceded to Aquinas it follows, logically and necessarily, that we end up with a notion of God which, while it is intelligible and comprehensible, is also, by the same token, a *finite* one.

11.3 Proof

Similar considerations would apply to the time-honoured, and sometimes impressive, attempts to prove the existence of God'. If God's existence could be proved, i.e., in *a logically rigorous fashion*, then we would
get, necessarily, a *finite* God – one which may be an essential *logical*
component in a speculative philosophical system but which cannot, in
principle, be the God of Abraham, Moses, Jesus, and Muhammad. No
amount of minute logic-chopping can advance the argument one little
bit. This consideration would apply equally, for instance, to Hartshorne's
formalisation of the revised second form of Anselm's ontological argument[4] as to the view of Peter Geach that in order to assess the validity
of the first three 'ways' of Aquinas we need to do 'a lot more hard logical work' since 'the formal logic of causal propositions, which was
studied a little in the Middle Ages, has made no progress to speak of
since then'.[5] It is interesting to note here that A. J. Ayer's attempt to
refute 'The claims of theology' (*The Central Questions of Philosophy*,
ch. X) makes much of the alleged proofs. But it must be allowed to
Ayer that if his approach to religion is cavalier then his *strictly logical*
arguments are cogent, and if he is evasive as regards the really profounder
aspects of religion then his case – on his own level – is elegant. In other
words, Ayer is in good company with Messrs Hartshorne and Geach,
among others, for they are playing exactly the same game, while quib-
bling a little about the interpretation of certain minor rules.[6]

In the same way we can extend the argument – i.e., the further implications of the logic of the infinite – and counter the idea that God
can be *known*, if only *indirectly*, *obliquely*, or even *symbolically*. So
also, we cannot, strictly speaking, say that God 'exists', or that He has
being or *reality*. In their different ways both Hepburn and Mascall (the
former a 'reverent agnostic', and the latter a prominent Anglo-Catholic)
miss the subtlety here. Hepburn writes: 'How God can be, but not by
being an individual entity, is profoundly obscure'; and in response to
the idea that God is 'above being': 'But in order to be "above", one must
first of all be – and continue to be' (*Encyclopaedia of Philosophy*, vol.
5, pp. 430, 431). Mascall develops a rather unsubtle and laboured 'Case
for Realism' as the basis of an argument for God's existence: 'This in-
built urge of the human mind to take all beings as its object and to press
beyond the horizon of the material world towards the realm of subsistent
being itself' (*The Openness of Being*, p. 100). Yet again, when the Sufis
assert that 'God is the sole Reality' and that, in consequence, the world
cannot have an independently real status, they are (1) equating God with

a finite concept *viz*. reality (even with a capital R), and (2) bracketing God and world within the same universe of discourse – thus 'God' is put in the same logical category as 'world', and is therefore a *finite* entity.

Chapter 12

The nature of our knowledge of God

12.1 Revelation: the terms predicated of God

> He is God besides Whom there is no God: The Knower of the unseen and the seen; He is the Beneficent, the Merciful.
>
> He is God, besides Whom there is no God; the King, the Holy, the Author of Peace, the Granter of Security, Guardian over all, the Mighty, the Supreme, the Possessor of greatness. Glory be to God from that which they set up with Him!
>
> He is God, the Creator, the Maker, the Fashioner: His are the most beautiful names. Whatever is in the heavens and the earth declares His glory; and He is the Mighty, the Wise.
>
> (Quran 59: 22, 23 and 24)

In what way do the terms predicated of God refer to Him? It is a direct consequence of the logic of the infinite that they cannot do so either straightforwardly or analogically. How then are we to understand them? Before we can begin to sketch out an answer we must distinguish between *God's Being* and *His Self-disclosure*. Clearly, by the logic of the infinite, 'God's Being' is a paradoxical expression. On the other hand, *God's Self-disclosure* is a perfectly plain formalisation of the fact that God makes Himself known to man in diverse ways: there is no paradox here; or, at any rate, the meaning of one part of this formalisation (the part pertaining to 'disclosure') is clear. Now God's Self-disclosure must clearly satisfy one condition: that it should be *intelligible* to man. The Self-disclosure must occur in a manner which *corresponds* to human understanding. Hence we may speak of *modes* of Divine Self-disclosure, and it follows that the criterion for their adequacy is the degree to which they actually correspond to the process of *human* understanding. So the most adequate mode of God's Self-disclosure to man must necessarily be the *human* mode. Therefore, the terms predicated of God must be taken *literally* – for they constitute *the human mode* of God's Self-disclosure. But since, by the logic of the infinite, they do not *refer* to God directly or indirectly, *there is no anthropomorphism*. Thus, for the Muslim, God reveals Himself in the Quran (the Word become Book), and for the Christian, God reveals Himself in Christ (the Word become Flesh): the two formulations being distinct species *under the one common genus of the human mode of God's Self-disclosure to man*.[1]

This very brief discussion is a tentative and schematic adumbration of a comprehensive theory of God's Self-revelation to man. It is, however, gratifying to note that it accords well with the position of al-Ghazali (see his formulation of the orthodox Muslim doctrine of God, section 7.2). Fazlur Rahman has stated it succinctly (*Islam*, p. 95):

> Fundamentally, al-Ghazali affirmed an agnosticism about the ultimate and absolute nature of God and maintained that He was knowable only in so far as He was related to and revealed Himself to man. This revealed and relational nature of God is constituted by the Divine Names and Attributes.

12.2 Religious experience: mysticism and epistemology

Ahmad Sirhindi (d. 1625), the great Indian Sufi, to whom reference was made earlier (section 11.1), developed a remarkably sophisticated analysis of mystical experience. He criticised and rejected Ibn al-Arabi's doctrine of *Wahdat al-Wujud* both on the very grounds on which the latter upheld it, *viz.* mystical experience, as well as on religious and metaphysical grounds. For him *wahi* or revelation was 'the criterion of the truth of mystic experience . . . . It says: . . . 'thy Lord is holier than the qualities which they ascribe to Him (37: 180)' (B. A. Faruqi, *The Mujaddid's Conception of Tawhid*, p. 101). Essentially he distinguishes between Oneness of Being proper (*Tawhid-i wujudi*), which he holds to be a speculative matter, as against Oneness as experienced (*Tawhid-i shuhudi*). The mystic's devotional and contemplative concentration on God is so intense that everything else fades out of his consciousness. 'This he calls (following al-Ghazali) *Shuhud* or experience (literally: "seeing" or "witnessing") and such unity is the Unity-in-experience (*Tawhid-i shuhudi*)' (F. Rahman, *Selected Letters of Shaikh Ahmad Sirhindi*, p. 44). However, Sirhindi maintains that it is wrong to speak, as the Sufis do, of an experience of God – for the Being and Attributes of God are beyond human comprehension. 'He the Holy One is beyond the Beyond, again beyond the Beyond, again beyond the Beyond' (Faruqi, *op. cit.*, p. 120). He therefore concludes that mystical experience is a purely subjective matter.

While we can disagree with Sirhindi's negative conclusion, there is no doubt that he had grasped the logic of the infinite. It is true that mystical experience is not in a straightforward sense 'an experience of God', but I suggest that it is one of the authentic modes of God's Self-disclosure. It is a sort of experiential analogue of the intellective understanding of the terms predicated of God. So, notwithstanding its very special qualities, it is a *finite human experience* (of the infinite). It is of considerable interest to note here that al-Ghazali was of the view that mystical experience revealed the true nature of the Divine Names and Attributes to man (see F. Rahman, *Islam*, p. 95).

If mystical experience is a finite human experience then it must be subject to the usual epistemological analysis of any kind of human experience. To say this is not, of course, to deny that it relates to an act of Divine Self-disclosure, but it does suggest that a lot of the current argument as to whether or not mystical experience is 'cognitive' misses the subtlety here. Thus R. W. Hepburn refers to Otto's parallel between musical experience and the experience of the numinous, and argues that 'The indescribability of some musical experience does not compel us to posit a mysterious other world of musical entities, to which music gives us access. One may ask: need the indescribability of *numinous* experience compel us any more to posit a transcendent source?' (in B. Mitchell (ed.), *The Philosophy of Religion*, pp. 176, 177). And further 'Neither felt uniqueness, degree of intensity, nor any other factor I can isolate in numinous experience guarantees that it is a veridical cognitive experience.' Now all this is perfectly true if we are thinking of God in terms of 'the existence of a transcendent being' (Hepburn, *op. cit.*, p. 177) — something which is ruled out by the logic of the infinite. It should therefore be possible to argue that mystical experience is cognitive not of 'God' but of the Self-disclosure of God *in a specific modality of human experience*. Of course it is true that this thesis can be sustained only within the living context of religion, i.e., within the context of an elaborate interpretative scheme.[2]

In the final analysis 'the living context of religion' implicates all the three great sources of our knowledge of God: revelation, reason and religious experience. The knowledge of God granted in revelation is understood, and partially confirmed, by reason, but its full nature is disclosed adequately only in the many varieties of religious experience. In the Muslim tradition al-Ghazali is the supreme exemplification of this process.

As W. H. T. Gairdner, the sensitive translator of his *Mishkat al-Anwar*, has put it: 'For him "Creed because Incredible" becomes "Gnosis because Agnoston".... What saved *God* for him from his obliterating agnosticism was the experience of the mystic leap, his own personal *mi'raj*' (*Mishkat al-Anwar*, p. 51). In al-Ghazali's own words: 'This did not come about by systematic demonstration or marshalled argument, but by a light which God most high cast into my breast. That light is the key to the greater part of knowledge.'[3]

Notes

Introduction

1   I am grateful to The Maulana Syed Abul Hasan Ali Nadwi for suggesting this idea to me in 1963.
2   *Islam*, London, 1966, pp. 224–5.
3   By 'the Indian subcontinent' I mean India, Pakistan and Bangladesh.
4   Khalifa Abdul Hakim, 'Renaissance in Indo-Pakistan: Iqbal', in M. M. Sharif (ed.), *A History of Muslim Philosophy*, Wiesbaden, 1966, vol. II, ch. LXXXII.
5   S. Alam Khundmiri, 'Conception of Time', in Hafeez Malik (ed.), *Iqbal: Poet-Philosopher of Pakistan*, Columbia, 1971, ch. 11, p. 243.
6   M. Iqbal, *The Reconstruction of Religious Thought in Islam*, Lahore, 1958, p. 7. The statement immediately following this one is noteworthy: I have quoted it on the title page of part I.
7   *Ibid.*, pp. v, vi.
8   See, for instance, A. Schimmel, *Gabriel's Wing*, Leiden, 1963, pp. 316, 321–2, 328, 330
9   Paradoxical, because Iqbal was an ardent admirer of the great seventeenth-century Indian Sufi Shaikh Ahmad Sirhindi, and there is some evidence to suggest that he followed the latter in rejecting the traditional Sufi teaching on God – the doctrine of Oneness of Being (*Wahdat al-Wujud*).

1   The arguments for the existence of god

1   Iqbal is, in fact, considering the modern versions of three of the *quinque viae* – the cosmological argument corresponding to *q.v.* (ii) (aetiological), the teleological argument corresponding to *q.v.* (v) (of the same name), and the ontological argument corresponding to *q.v.* (iii) (cosmological).

2 In this connection the following crucial statement (apropos al-
Ghazali's view of knowledge and intuition) is also noteworthy. This
text is decisive in regard to the question of an Hegelian influence
(pp. 6-7):

> In its deeper movement, however, thought is capable of reaching
> an immanent Infinite in whose self-unfolding movement the
> various finite concepts are merely moments. In its essential
> nature, then, thought is not static; it is dynamic and unfolds its
> internal infinitude in time like the seed which, from the very
> beginning, carries within itself the organic unity of the tree as a
> present fact. Thought is, therefore, the whole in its dynamic
> self-expression, appearing to the temporal vision as a series of
> definite specifications which cannot be understood except by a
> reciprocal reference. Their meaning lies not in their self-identity,
> but in the larger whole of which they are the specific aspects.
> This larger whole is, to use a Quranic metaphor, a kind of
> 'Preserved Tablet', which holds up the entire undetermined pos-
> sibilities of knowledge as a present reality, revealing itself in
> serial time as a succession of finite concepts appearing to reach a
> unity which is already present in time. It is in fact the presence
> of the total Infinite in the movement of knowledge that makes
> finite thinking possible. Both Kant and Ghazali failed to see that
> thought, in the very act of knowledge, passes beyond its own
> finitude. The finitudes of Nature are reciprocally exclusive. Not
> so the finitudes of thought which is, in its essential nature, in-
> capable of limitation and cannot remain imprisoned in the
> narrow circuit of its own individuality. In the wide world
> beyond itself nothing is alien to it. It is in its progressive partici-
> pation in the life of the apparently alien that thought demolishes
> the walls of its finitude and enjoys its potential infinitude. Its
> movement becomes possible only because of the implicit
> presence in its finite individuality of the infinite, which keeps
> alive within it the flame of aspiration and sustains it in its end-
> less pursuit. It is a mistake to regard thought as inconclusive, for
> it too, in its own way, is a greeting of the finite with the infinite.

2 Hegel

1 'But if Hegelian "science" is marked by an unprecedented philosophical presumptuousness it is also marked by an equally unprecedented philosophical humility, and only if both are seen together
is there any hope of doing justice to either' E. L. Fackenheim,
The Religious Dimension in Hegel's Thought, Indiana, 1967, p. 33.
2 See Fackenheim, *op. cit.*, p. 110.

3 (a) See Heidegger's opening note in his *Hegel's Concept of Experience*, New York, 1970, pp. 7, 13. (b) 'The wealth of human experience actually described in *The Phenomenology of Spirit* is a most eloquent demonstration that Hegel's method is far more "empirical" than that of philosophers who call themselves "empiricists"', K. R. Dove, *The Review of Metaphysics*, vol. 23, no. 4, June 1970, p. 624.

4 'What logic is cannot be stated beforehand, rather does this knowledge of what it is first emerge as the final outcome and consummation of the whole exposition . . . the Notion of logic has its genesis in the course of the exposition', *The Science of Logic*, trans. A. V. Miller, London, 1969, p. 43.

5 The matter has been put very well by Lauer: ' "The philosophy of religion" of which Hegel speaks is not a philosophising about religion; it is the thinking philosophically what religion thinks religiously'. See Q. Lauer, 'Hegel on the identity of content in religion and philosophy', in D. E. Christensen (ed.), *Hegel and the Philosophy of Religion*, The Hague, 1970, section viii, p. 273.

6 'Thought "overreaches and comprehends (*übergreift*)" being', G. Mure, *The Philosophy of Hegel*, London, 1965, p. 9.

7 'This challenging and controversial book is the most important work on Hegel's treatment of religion to appear in English', K. L. Schmitz, *The Review of Metaphysics*, vol. 23, no. 4, June 1970, p. 721.

8 This particular Hegelian insight has a remarkable but hitherto unrecognised affinity with the philosophies of both Husserl and Heidegger. This appears to be a major intersection in modern thought and one with momentous consequences for the understanding of the problem of knowledge.

3 Science

1 It would be far less problematical if time was conceived of as an element (or phenomenon) disclosed in experience.

2 (a) The word 'experience' is in any case an ambiguous one. Note the fine linguistic point made by Findlay: 'the English word is used in two ways, clear in the context, and it is in fact practically two words. "Having an experience" and "learning by experience" obviously involve two distinct, though cognate, uses of the word "experience"', E. Husserl, *Logical Investigations*, trans. J. N. Findlay, London, 1980, p. 39.
(b) However, it is a weighty word. To ask a philosopher to spell out his concept of *'experience'* is tantamount to demanding at least the basic epistemological and ontological elements of his world-view. Consider in this context the Whiteheadian criticism about the unempirical character of the Humean school (Dorothy Emmet's

A. N. Whitehead); Merleau-Ponty's characterisation of phenomenology as 'a direct description of our experience as it is' (preface to *Phenomenology of Perception*); and again Heidegger's view of *Hegel's Concept of Experience* (see his book of that title). The seemingly simple word 'experience' clearly bears abundant philosophical riches.

(c) Finally, I would venture the remark that while such an acute mind in the analytic tradition as W. V. O. Quine has made some interesting remarks about 'experience' (see for instance, 'Studies in the Theory of Knowledge', *American Philosophical Quarterly*, Monograph 4, Oxford, 1970, p. 43), the word has received its fullest and deepest meaning in the phenomenology of Edmund Husserl (see, for instance, his exquisitely subtle work *Experience and Judgement*, Evanston, 1973).

3 For the origins of the theory see A. N. Whitehead's *The Concept of Nature*, Cambridge, 1971, ch. 2.

4 Iqbal is quoting here but does not give the source of his quotation.

5 Again, Iqbal is quoting but the source of this quotation is not given. It is probably taken from Russell's *The ABC of Relativity*, London, 1958.

6 I am much indebted to my friend, Dr J. N. Islam, late of the Institute of Theoretical Astronomy, Cambridge, and now Reader in Mathematics, City University, London, for an extended and illuminating discussion of this problem.

7 Even as metaphysical a contemporary philosopher as Errol E. Harris can declare that 'The truth, the disclosure of the actual nature of the real, is the ultimate goal of science, for the achievement of which perceptual experience is examined, analysed, ordered and systematised', *The Foundations of Metaphysics in Science*, London, 1965, p. 492.

8 I owe this expressive phrase, which conjures up the picture of a corresponding visual model, to my teacher in the philosophy of science, Professor R. B. Braithwaite.

4 Bergson

1 So far there has been only one reference to the Quran, *viz.* 'The clue furnished by the Quran' (see p. 6) and one to the tradition of Muslim thought. From this point onward, however, substantial reference is made to the Quran and the Islamic tradition and it will be convenient to deal with all these references in one section later on.

2 For the sake of brevity and clarity I have been schematic, perhaps even dogmatic, in this preliminary statement. Contemporary discussion of this problem has become a highly complicated matter. I

wish to enter a caveat here. It is my impression that insufficient attention has been paid to the distinct nature of Aristotelian final causality and teleology in the sense I have defined it; failure to make this distinction leads to much confusion. This consideration is particularly relevant in the context of Bergson.

3 In this part of our brief survey I have not really distinguished between teleology in individual human life as against teleology in the whole evolutionary process. Bergson's discussion cuts across both.

4 At least those writings available to Iqbal up to 1928/9, when his lectures were delivered.

5 Conclusions and critique

1 Note, for instance: 'Thus a comprehensive philosophical criticism of all the facts of experience . . . brings us to the conclusion that the ultimate Reality is a rationally directed creative life' (see section 5.3, p. 36).

6 Iqbal and the Quran

1 (a) Some verses, e.g., 39:5 and 23:80, have been quoted only in part by Iqbal. (b) There are mistakes, and misprints, in numbering. (c) I give Muhammad Ali's translation, but I follow Iqbal in translating *Allah* as God.

2 See *The Tarjuman al-Quran*, London, 1962, vol. 1, especially pp. 13, 31, 32, 34, 35, 39, 47, 48, 49.

3 Schuon has also pointed out that the identical word *ayāt* (signs) is used for both the *verses* of the Quran as well as the *signs* of nature, and this symbolises the parallelism of revelation and nature.

7 Muslim theism: the classical formulation of the orthodox doctrine by al-Ghazali and Abul-Kalam Azad

1 True reason − as a God-given faculty − points in the direction of God. It is 'the spark in our clod, our native orientation to the divine' (Bernard Lonergan, *Method in Theology*, London, 1972, p. 103).

2 The late Professor A. J. Arberry of Cambridge, who, incidentally, was one of the very few western scholars to recognise the truly Islamic origins of Sufism, writes of al-Ghazali: 'Yet despite his celebrity and authority − his work as a lawyer in particular qualified him to be called the greatest Shafii jurisconsult after Al-Shafi himself − he was dissatisfied with the intellectual and legalistic approach to religion, and felt a yearning for a more personal experience of God' (*Sufism*, London, 1950, p. 79).

3 This quotation, from al-Ghazali's monumental work *The Revival of the Religious Sciences*, is extracted from a longer one in Hartshorne and Reese, *Philosophers Speak of God*, Chicago, 1953, p. 107. They include him in their chapter on 'Classical Theism'. The full statement by al-Ghazali is given in Margaret Smith's *Al-Ghazali*, London, 1944, pp. 133–5.

4 Specifically in section VI 'The Quranic Concept of God: a Comparative Study', which constitutes Azad's commentary on the fourth verse: 'Thee alone do we serve, and Thee alone do we ask for help' (*The Tarjuman al-Quran*, vol. I).

8 Muslim pantheism: the modernist 'reconstruction' of the Quranic doctrine by Muhammad Iqbal

1 A finite deity may be defined as one which partakes, in some fundamental respect, of the limited and imperfect character of the order of nature.

2 See Alasdair McIntyre, *The Encyclopaedia of Philosophy*, vol. 6, article on 'Pantheism'. For definitions of pantheism see also H. P. Owen, *Concepts of Deity*, and E. G. Parrinder, 'Definitions of Mysticism'.

3 See, for instance, the section on Iqbal in Hartshorne and Reese, *Philosophers Speak of God*. The two notions of pantheism and panentheism are so intimately related that it may not always be easy to draw a line between them. Pantheism, in the simplest terms, may be defined as the idea of a straightforward identity of God and world, whereas panentheism is the notion of God as including, but also transcending, the world. H. P. Owen has argued that the normal definition of panentheism applies to many pantheists as well, to the extent that the latter make some concession to the notion of God's transcendence (*Concepts of Deity*, London, 1971, pp. 74, 75).

4 Alternative terms used by Iqbal are: the Divine Self, the Ultimate Self or Ego, the Ultimate Reality, the Centralising Ego, the Creative Self, the Immanent Self.

5 This important term has been variously translated, and usually quite misleadingly. In this work I have adopted the translation of Martin Lings in his *A Sufi Saint of the Twentieth Century* (London, 1971).

6 (a) Of particular interest here is R. C. Whittemore's view of 'Hegel as Panentheist', an impressive piece of carefully considered argument (*Tulane Studies in Philosophy*, vol. IX).
(b) Consider also the observation of James Collins that 'Hegel often denies that his philosophy is pantheistic. He distinguishes between a vulgar pantheism and a more sophisticated sort.' Collins's own

111

thesis is that 'Hegel's theory is neither Christian nor theistic, neither pantheistic nor atheistic, but a distinctive monism of absolute spirit', *God in Modern Philosophy*, London, 1960, pp. 235, 435, n.34.

(c) It is highly probable that Iqbal (especially in view of his Cambridge period with McTaggart) was influenced by McTaggart's interpretations of Hegel. See, for instance, McTaggart, *Studies in Hegelian Philosophy*, Cambridge, 1918, ch. III, 'On the personality of the absolute'.

(d) Hegel himself would probably argue that *all* of these seemingly distinct positions should properly be seen as 'moments in the dialectical unfolding of Absolute Spirit'.

7 'God as Eternal-Temporal Consciousness, Knowing and Including the World in His Own Actuality (but Not in His Essence).'

8 If one was to continue the Iqbalian enterprise today, presumably one would have to read into these verses Husserlian analyses of 'Internal Time-Consciousness' (*inneren Zeitbewusstseins*) or whatever other theory of time is currently in fashion.

9 See note 3 of this chapter.

10 See Abu Sayeed Nur-ud-din, 'Attitude toward Sufism', in H. Malik (ed.), *Iqbal*, New York, 1971, ch. 13.

9 Muslim pantheism: the contemporary exposition of the Sufi doctrine by Isa Nuruddin (Schuon) and Abubakr Sirajuddin (Lings)

1 Both Isa Nuruddin and Abubakr Sirajuddin usually write under their European names – hence I have adhered to their own practice in the course of my discussion.

2 (a) See note 5 of chapter 8.

(b) The consideration of the Sufi doctrine leads on, quite naturally, to the problem of mystical experience and its conceptual interpretation. The discussion of this issue of experience and interpretation (chapter 10) centres around the work of the contemporary philosopher W. T. Stace.

3 Venerated by Sufis as *al-Shaikh al-Akbar* (or the Greatest Doctor); 'the greatest mystical genius of the Arabs' – A. J. Arberry (*Sufism*, p. 97). But, at the same time, 'Some whole books or chapters of books have been written in defence of his orthodoxy or against his alleged heterodoxy . . . . There has never been in the whole history of Islam another man whose faith has been so much in question' A. E. Affifi, in Sharif, M. M. (ed.), *A History of Muslim Philosophy*, Wiesbaden, 1963, vol. 1, pp. 398, 405.

4 *Despite* my critical analysis, I would emphasise that I have found much illumination in his writings – they are quite remarkable for their originality and spiritual depth. I regard Monsieur Schuon's

writings as a most worthy and substantial answer to the ever present, and pressing, need to expound the authentic mystical understanding and interpretation of the Muslim faith. His contribution has a particular, and poignant, relevance to Muslims today in view of the profound, and perhaps unprecedented, spiritual disorientation and dislocation in which they find themselves. My critique should be read in the context of these remarks.

5 The rhetoric – possibly of Neoplatonic origin – about 'the Principle, which is both Being and Beyond-Being' and 'formal and supra-formal' manifestation can be ignored (see R. T. Wallis, *Neoplatonism*). Similarly, the irrelevant reference to Eckhart: 'the Godhead' (*Gottheit*) is simply the Christian notion of God as undifferentiated into the Trinity (see W. T. Stace, *Mysticism and Philosophy*, and H. P. Owen, *Concepts of Deity*).

6 See notes 2 and 3 of chapter 8.

7 There may quite possibly be a Neoplatonic influence here (*via* Ibn al-Arabi). The subsequent elaboration, however, betrays a clear Hindu origin.

8 This is not to say that the great religions are not all *symbolisations* of some 'One Ultimate Truth', but rather that there is no easy way of showing the relationship between, or equivalence of, the different symbols.

9 This critical appraisal (of the substance of chapter V) should in no way detract from the value of Dr Lings's book as a whole, It is, in fact, an important and distinguished contribution to the scanty literature on Sufism. Particularly outstanding is the way in which Doctor Lings's account of Sufism revolves so successfully around the life and teaching of a great, but not hitherto widely known, contemporary Sufi master; this gives his work a vibrant, living quality.

10 Lings's manifest keenness and anxiety lead him to the implausible extreme of ascribing the Oneness of Being doctrine even to Christian mysticism (p. 124).

11 More generally, of course, the Quran claims to be the perfection of *all* previous religious teaching.

12 Also known by several other names, among them: *Umm al-Kitab* ('the Essence of the Divine Writ'), and *Asas al-Quran* ('the Foundation of the Quran'). See Muhammad Asad, *The Message of the Quran.*

13 I give Muhammad Ali's translation, but follow Lings in translating *Allah* as God.

14 The *Taj al-Arus* (Dictionary) by Imam Muhibb al-Din Abu-l-Faid Murtada, and E. W. Lane's *Arabic English Lexicon.*

15 'Holy Tradition' – *Hadith Qudsi*: those traditions in which God speaks in the first person through the Prophet. There are forty of these in all.

16 Muhammad Asad's translation; he comments on this verse in a penetrating note: 'the term *latif* denotes something that is extremely
subtle in quality, and therefore immaterial, intangible or unfathomable. Whenever this term occurs in the *Quran* with reference to
God in conjunction with the adjective *khabir* ('all-aware'), it is in-
variably used to express the idea of His inaccessibility to human
perception, imagination or comprehension, as contrasted with His
all-awareness (see, apart from the above verse, also 22:63, 31:16,
33:34 and 67:14). In the two instances where the combination of
latif and *khabir* carries the definite article *al* (6:103 and 67:14),
the expression *huwa 'l-latif* has the meaning of 'He *alone* is unfathomable' – implying that this quality of His is unique and
absolute, *The Meaning of the Quran*, Gibraltar, 1980, pp. 188 n.89.
17 Muhammad Ali translates and comments on this verse on essentially the same lines, *The Holy Quran*, Lahore, 1951, p. 370, n.995.
18 Fazlur Rahman has shown how the orthodox Muslim doctrine
may, if taken too far in the direction of the supreme and absolute
transcendence of God, lead to the Oneness of Being doctrine. Thus,
the Sunni theology of al-Ashari declared that the sole author of all
acts was God, and Sufi theosophy transformed this into 'nothing
exists except Allah', *Islam*, London, 1966, p. 141.
19 I am not examining Gairdner's case in detail, as a more rigorous,
and philosophically more sophisticated analysis can be made
directly of al-Ghazali's own text.
20 This point was brought home to me in a personal discussion with
Dr Lings. He said, with reference to Ahmad Sirhindi's rejection of
the Oneness of Being doctrine: 'Perhaps his experience did not
correspond to *Wahdat al-Wujud*.'

10 Mystical experience and interpretation

1 Findlay's idea of 'The Logic of Mysticism' is absurd, since it
implies some autonomous system of logic. Strictly speaking, this
notion is not even intelligible. By what *logical* criteria could such a
postulated or, more accurately, fantasised, logic be judged?
2 This very simple model corresponds roughly to Edmund Husserl's
threefold division: (1) pre-predicative experience, (2) predicative
thought, and (3) general, conceptual thought. (See his great work
Experience and Judgement, Evanston, 1973.)
3 See chapter 8, notes 2 and 3 of this book.
4 (a) Alasdair MacIntyre has also remarked that it is noteworthy how
often pantheism is linked to mystical and contemplative doctrines
and practice (*Encyclopaedia of Philosophy*, 1967, vol. 6,
'Pantheism').
(b) Commenting on the fact that mystical experiences themselves

can be interpreted differently, R. W. Hepburn writes: 'The choice between pantheism and theism is a choice between two massive conceptual systems', *Encyclopaedia of Philosophy*, 1967, vol. 5, p. 430.

5 In the Muslim tradition one could mention the names of Ibn al-Arabi, al-Ghazali, and Ahmad Sirhindi as major theorists, i.e. over and above their actual mystical practice and experience.

11 The logic of the infinite

1 Again, in relation to the question of proving the existence of God, H. D. Lewis observes, subtly, as follows (pp. 157–8):

> But alas religious truth is not of this order. It is in some respects simple, but this is not at any level the simplicity of a trim argument. We should understand by now why this is so. At the centre of religion is the idea of a transcendent or Absolute Being, who, from the nature of the case, is beyond the sphere in which we relate things rationally to one another. He is beyond the unity of system as we know it, and thus it is out of the question to know Him by argument of any kind.

2 To adopt Frege's distinction, this term has sense but no reference.
3 A. Kenny (ed.), *Aquinas*, part 1 ('Logic and Metaphysics'), 'Analogy as a rule of meaning for religious language'. The formulation of the two rules of 'Analogy of attribution' and 'Analogy of proper proportionality' takes up almost forty pages, and this is followed by a brief sketch (six pages) showing their application to language about God.
4 (a) John Hick, 'Ontological argument for the existence of God', *Encyclopaedia of Philosophy*, 1967, vol. 5. (b) This argument, incidentally, was formulated by a Muslim philosopher *before* Anselm: see Parwez Morewedge, 'Avicenna on the ontological argument', *The Monist*, April 1970.
5 *God and the Soul*, 1969, as quoted by E. L. Mascall in *The Openness of Being*, London, 1971, pp. 110–12.
6 The current renewed interest in these arguments may, in the long term, prove to be no more than the desperate last-ditch stand of one of the subtler forms of neo-positivism in religious thought.

12 The nature of our knowledge of God

1 As a committed Muslim I am bound to say that my position *appears, prima facie*, to be somewhat embarrassing in terms of its implications for me of the Christian doctrine of the incarnation.

115

This might, for instance, *appear* to be its logical conclusion. This does not, I believe, necessarily follow.

2 This way of approaching the problem may provide one solution to the vexed question of relating non-theistic (for example, the Buddhist experience of *nirvana*) to theistic forms of mysticism.

3 W. Montgomery Watt, *The Faith and Practice of al-Ghazali*, London, 1953, p. 25. Montgomery Watt observes sympathetically, and acutely, that: 'Islam is now wrestling with Western thought as it once wrestled with Greek philosophy, and is as much in need as it was then of a "revival of the religious sciences". Deep study of al-Ghazali may suggest to Muslims steps to be taken if they are to deal successfully with the contemporary situation.'

Bibliography

Islam

Quran

Asad, M., *The Message of the Quran*, Gibraltar, 1980.
Azad, A. K., *The Tarjuman al-Quran*, London, 1962, vol. 1.
Muhammad Ali, *The Holy Quran*, Lahore, 1951.
Rahman, F., *Islam*, London, 1966, ch. 2, 'The Quran'.
Schuon, F., *Understanding Islam*, London, ch. 2, 'The Quran'.

Iqbal

Hakim, K. A., 'Renaissance in Indo-Pakistan: Iqbal', in M.M. Sharif (ed.) *A History of Muslim Philosophy*, Wiesbaden, 1966, vol. 2, ch. 82.
Iqbal, M., *The Reconstruction of Religious Thought in Islam*, Lahore, 1958.
Khatoon, J., *The Place of God, Man and Universe in the Philosophic System of Iqbal*, Karachi, 1963.
Malik, H. (ed.), *Iqbal*, New York, 1971.
Schimmel, A., *Gabriel's Wing*, Leiden, 1963.
Siddiqi, M., *Concept of Muslim Culture in Iqbal*, Islamabad, 1970.
Various authors, *Iqbal as Thinker*, Lahore, 1952.

Other Works

Arberry, A. J., *Sufism*, London, 1950.
Faruqi, B. A., *The Mujaddid's Conception of Tawhid*, Lahore, 1940.
Friedmann, Y., *Shaykh Ahmad Sirhindi*, Montreal, 1971.
Al-Ghazali, *Mishkat al-Anwar*, trans. W. H. T. Gairdner, Lahore, 1952.
Lings, M., *A Sufi Saint of the Twentieth Century*, London, 1971.

Bibliography

Morewedge, P., 'Avicenna on the ontological argument', *Monist*, April 1970.
Rahman, F., *Islam*, London, 1966.
Rahman, F., *Selected Letters of Shaikh Ahmad Sirhindi*, Karachi, 1968.
Rahman, F., 'Islamic Thought in the Indo-Pakistan Sub-Continent and the Middle East', unpublished manuscript, 1971.
Schuon, F., *The Transcendent Unity of Religions*, London, 1953.
Schuon, F., *Understanding Islam*, London, 1963.
Sharif, M. M., *A History of Muslim Philosophy*, 2 vols, Wiesbaden, 1963, 1966.
Smith, M., *Al-Ghazali: The Mystic*, London, 1944.
Watt, W. M., *The Faith and Practice of Al-Ghazali*, London, 1953.
Watt, W. M., *Al-Ghazali, The Encyclopaedia of Islam*, Leiden, 1965, new edn, vol. 2, pp. 1038-41.

Western Thought

Philosophy of Religion

Ayer, A. J., 'The Claims of theology', in *The Central Questions of Philosophy*, London, 1973, ch. x.
Collins, J., *God in Modern Philosophy*, London, 1960.
Findlay, J. N., *Ascent to the Absolute*, London, 1970, ch. x, 'The Logic of Mysticism'.
Garside, B., 'Language and the interpretation of mystical experience', *Int. J. Phil. of Rel.*, vol. III, no. 2, 1972, pp. 93-102.
Hartshorne, C. and Reese, W. L., *Philosophers Speak of God*, Chicago, 1953.
Hepburn, R. W., 'Religious experience: argument for the existence of god', *Encyclopaedia of Philosophy*, 1967, vol. 7.
Hepburn, R. W., 'Mysticism, nature and assessment of', *Encyclopaedia of Philosophy*, 1967, vol. 5.
Hick, J., 'Ontological argument for the existence of God', *Encyclopaedia of Philosophy*, 1967, vol. 5.
Kenny, A. (ed.), *Aquinas*, London, 1969.
Lewis, H. D., *Philosophy of Religion*, London, 1965.
Lonergan, B., *Method in Theology*, London, 1972.
MacIntyre, A., 'Pantheism', *Encyclopaedia of Philosophy*, 1967, vol. 6.
Mascall, E. L., *He Who Is*, London, 1966.
Mascall, E. L., *The Openness of Being*, London, 1971.
Mitchell, B. (ed.), *Philosophy of Religion*, Oxford, 1971.
Owen, H. P., *Concepts of Deity*, London, 1971.
Parrinder, E. G., 'Definitions of Mysticism', *Ex Orbe Religionum*, Studies for G. Widengren, Leiden, 1972, pp. 307-17.

Smart, N., 'Interpretation and religious experience', *Rel. Stud.*, vol. I, 1965, pp. 75-87.

Smart, N., *Philosophers and Religious Truth*, London, 1969.

Smart, N., *The Concept of Worship*, London, 1972.

Stace, W. T., *Mysticism and Philosophy*, London, 1961.

Zaehner, R. C., *Mysticism: Sacred and Profane*, Oxford, 1957.

Hegel

Christensen, D. E., *Hegel and the Philosophy of Religion*, The Hague, 1970.

Collins, J., 'God and the Hegelian Absolute'. *God in Modern Philosophy*, London, 1960, ch. VII.

Dove, K. R., 'Hegel's phenomenological method', in *The Review of Metaphysics*, vol. 23, no. 4, 1970.

Fackenheim, E. L., *The Religious Dimension in Hegel's Thought*, Indiana, 1967.

Hegel, G. W. F., 'Lectures on the Proofs of the Existence of God', *Hegel's Lectures on the Philosophy of Religion*, vol. III, London, 1895.

Hegel, G. W. F., *The Science of Logic*, trans. A. V. Miller, London, 1969.

Hegel, G. W. F., *The Logic of Hegel*, trans. W. Wallace, Oxford, 1892.

Heidegger, M., *Hegel's Concept of Experience*, New York, 1970.

Kaufmann, W., *Hegel*, London, 1966.

McTaggart, J. M. E., *Studies in Hegelian Dialectic*, Cambridge, 1918.

Mure, G. R. G., *An Introduction to Hegel*, Oxford, 1940.

Mure, G. R. G., *The Philosophy of Hegel*, London, 1965.

Schmitz, K. L., 'Hegel's Philosophy of Religion: typology and strategy', *Review of Metaphysics*, vol. 23, no. 4, 1970.

Soll, I., *An Introduction to Hegel's Metaphysics*, Chicago, 1969.

Whittemore, R. C., 'Hegel as panentheist', *Tulane Studies in Philosophy*, vol. IX, 1960.

Bergson

Beckner, M. O., 'Teleology', *Encyclopaedia of Philosophy*, 1967, vol. 8.

Bergson, H., *Time and Free Will*, London, 1910.

Bergson, H., *Matter and Memory*, London, 1911.

Bergson, H., *Introduction to Metaphysics*, London, 1913.

Bergson, H., *Life and Consciousness*, Birmingham, 1914.

Bergson, H., *Mind-Energy*, London, 1920.

Bergson, H., *Creative Evolution*, London, 1960.

Collingwood, R. G., *The Idea of Nature*, Oxford, 1965, part III, section I.2.

Bibliography

Goudge, T. A., 'H. Bergson', *Encyclopaedia of Philosophy*, 1967, vol. 1.
Merleau-Ponty, M., *In Praise of Philosophy, Evanston*, 1963, section II.
Russell, B., *H. Bergson*, Cambridge, 1914.

Other Works

Einstein, A., *Relativity*, London, 1957.
Emmet, D., *Whitehead's Philosophy of Organism*, London, 1932.
Emmet, D., *A. N. Whitehead*, London, 1949.
Emmet, D., 'A. N. Whitehead', *Encyclopaedia of Philosophy*, 1967, vol. 8.
Findlay, J. N., translator's introduction to Edmund Husserl's *Logical Investigations*, London, 1970.
Grünbaum, A., 'Philosophical significance of relativity theory', *Encyclopaedia of Philosophy*, 1967, vol. 7.
Grünbaum, A., *Modern Science and Zeno's Paradoxes*, London, 1968.
Grünbaum, A., *Philosophical Problems of Space and Time*, New York, 1963.
Guthrie, W. K. C., *A History of Greek Philosophy*, London, 1969, vol. II.
Harris, E. E., *Nature, Mind and Modern Science*, London, 1954.
Harris, E. E., *The Foundations of Metaphysics in Science*, London, 1965.
Husserl, E., *Experience and Judgement*, Evanston, 1973.
Jonas, H., *The Phenomenon of Life*, New York, 1966.
Morgenbesser, S. (ed.), *Philosophy of Science Today*, New York, 1967.
Quine, W. V. O., 'Studies in the theory of knowledge', *American Philosophical Quarterly*, Monograph 4, Oxford, 1970, p. 43.
Russell, B., *The ABC of Relativity*, London, 1958, rev. edn.
Vlastos, G., 'Zeno of Elea', *Encyclopaedia of Philosophy*, 1967, vol. 8.
Wallis, R. T., *Neoplatonism*, London, 1972.
Whitehead, A. N., *Science and the Modern World*, New York, 1948.
Whitehead, A. N., *The Concept of Nature*, Cambridge, 1971.
Whitehead, A. N., *The Principles of Natural Knowledge*, Cambridge, 1919.

Index

121

Index

MORE ABOUT KPI BOOKS

If you would like further information about books available from KPI please write to

> The Marketing Department
> KPI Limited
> Routledge & Kegan Paul plc
> 14 Leicester Square
> London WC2H 7PH

In the USA write to

> The Marketing Department
> KPI Limited
> Routledge & Kegan Paul
> 29 West 35th Street,
> New York
> N.Y. 10001, USA

In Australia write to

> The Marketing Department
> KPI Limited
> Routledge & Kegan Paul
> c/o Methuen Law Book Company
> 44 Waterloo Road
> North Ryde, NSW 2113
> Australia

KPI